From
Power
to
Peace

"Family" gained a whole new meaning for the Magruders after the Watergate trauma and Jeb's seven-month separation from his wife, Gail, and the four children: Whitney, 17; Justin, 15; Tracy, 13; Stuart, 11. *Paul Rey photo*

Jeb Stuart Magruder

From Power to Peace

Foreword by
Senator Mark O. Hatfield

WORD BOOKS
PUBLISHER
WACO, TEXAS

I would like to thank . . .
Linda Daniell, Char Meredith, and Jim Nordby of
Young Life for their help and encouragement while
we were at work on this book. Eloise Hatfield of
Campus Crusade for Christ for her stimulating
suggestions and criticism along the way.

FROM POWER TO PEACE
Copyright © 1978 by Jeb Stuart Magruder

Fictional names have been given to some of the people
in this book to protect them from embarrassment or
danger.

The quotation from *A New Joy* (© Fleming H.
Revell, 1973) by Colleen Evans is used by
permission of the publisher.
Jacket photo by Paul Rey.

Library of Congress Catalog Card Number: 77-92464

ISBN 0-8499-0074-3

Printed in the United States of America

For my children

Whitney, Justin, Tracy, and Stuart

With grateful appreciation to Laura
Hobe, whose editorial assistance has
proved invaluable to the writer.

Contents

Foreword by Senator Mark Hatfield

Key Persons

Chronology of Events

1. My Double Life   *21*

2. Don't Tell the Truth   *45*

3. Louie   *64*

4. Daddy, Why Do You Have to Go to Prison?   *79*

5. Allenwood   *98*

6. View from the Inside   *113*

7. Letters from Home   *134*

8. Watch Out for Carl   *147*

9. Fort Holabird   *159*

10. The Watergate Trial   *176*

11. On the Outside   *187*

12. Young Life   *204*

I want to express my appreciation to all those Washington friends who stood with us in the hectic days there following the Watergate revelations . . . our friends across the country who continued to show their concern for us . . . and our friends in Colorado Springs who have been so supportive. Unfortunately, it has been impossible to mention all of them in the book—but they know who they are and how much we appreciate them.

Foreword

Jeb Magruder was barely an acquaintance of mine during the time of President Nixon's reelection in 1972, and in the initial Watergate aftermath which followed. He was just another publicly well-known personality on what was, in some sense, the other side. Though I am a fellow Republican, I was on one of the enemies' lists issued from the White House. My relationships with the close allies of the President during that time were often distant and strained. Jeb Magruder had never been a political associate, companion, or ally of mine. In short, there was no normal reason for me to feel any sense of affinity with him.

Our friendship started when Jeb was in the midst

of his fall from power, as Watergate unfolded and claimed its victims. Its beginning, in fact, was totally nonpolitical—our wives were in a group that met for fellowship and prayer. But from then and to this day, what has transpired within the life of Jeb Magruder has made a profound and lasting impression upon me.

Jeb Magruder was close to the vortex of political power in Washington; he ran the day-by-day details of President Nixon's reelection campaign, headed Nixon's Inaugural, and was regarded as a rising young star among Washington's politically influential personalities. But within the course of a few months, he found himself in federal prison. Probably that is what you know and remember about him from reading newspaper stories during those years.

In *From Power to Peace,* however, Jeb Magruder tells what is to me a far more fascinating, dramatic and significant story—what went on within his own life. And he does this with a disarming and unrestrained candor. He is candid about himself, about fellow Watergate conspirators like John Dean, H. R. Haldeman, John Mitchell, and others. He is also candid about Richard Nixon, the Watergate prosecutors, prison life, our nation's system of criminal justice, politics, his own family, and his personal faith.

Watergate was rooted in deception, dishonesty, and face-saving ambition, a process in which Magruder, by his own admission, played a large role. The power of this book, by contrast, is its openness, its forthrightness, its humility, and its honesty. It is refreshing and salutary to read such words from a man like Jeb Magruder. More important, the account stands out as a testimony to the spiritual transformation which has occurred in his own life.

You will not find even a hint of self-justification

in this book. Jeb Magruder acknowledges the wrong in his participation in the Watergate cover-up, and he is free to say so in ways that are not calculated to evoke pity. He writes neither to be recognized as a martyr nor to gain some public reprieve for his actions. This in itself is a refreshing departure from many of the post-Watergate chronicles written by its various participants.

The heart of Jeb Magruder's story, however, is his personal discovery of faith in Jesus Christ, and his decision to orient his life as one of Christ's followers. Here again, what is remarkable is the candor with which Jeb relates his journey. This is no "from drunk to saint" testimony. Rather, the real struggles of Jeb's pilgrimage in his faith are laid out for us all to share. And in this sharing of his humanity, Jeb Magruder's journey should find deep points of identification with each of our lives.

The discovery of evangelical Christianity by the secular media in the past couple of years has tended to make celebrities out of new converts who previously were well-known to the public from politics, entertainment, or sports. There is a danger in this trend; being born again can be reduced to the level of looking like a popular fad, and the full meaning of following Christ in all of life can be overlooked and ignored. There is also a danger to the particular "celebrities" who are chosen by the Christian community for its admiration; a new form of pride, ambition, and face-saving may be nurtured in them as an unintended result.

Jeb Magruder has become aware of these dangers, and this sensitivity is reflected in his book. The relating of his personal faith rings with integrity because it is filled with the realities of an openly revealed life. The dehumanizing pressures of prison, the threatening questions of identity and vocation, and the particular temptations and disillusionments which he found within the Christian community all are unfolded with the story of his growing faith.

This is no picture of a life to be placed on a pedestal. This is the last thing Jeb Magruder would want. Rather, there is the clear presentation of what it has meant, and continues to mean, for the life of this particular individual to be reoriented around the person of Jesus Christ.

When history is written, the sweep of dramatic public events becomes the focus of attention. During the Watergate years of 1973 and 1974, the newspaper exposures, the congressional hearings, the grand jury indictments, the impeachment proceedings, and the resignation of Richard Nixon were set forth as the most historic happenings of those days.

But there is another history of that time which revolves around the inner lives of those caught up in this sweep of events. In the case of Jeb Magruder, this history is every bit as important and revealing. It shows us how those faulty attitudes, values, and ambitions which were at the core of Watergate can be overcome in the lives of individuals through the experience of a personal and vital faith. This is a history which urgently needs to be known.

Watergate was not merely the result of the sins of individuals. It revealed to us dimensions of political corruption within our whole political system, as Magruder's account makes clear. But the foremost truth this book communicates is the fact that a life subtly dominated by the ways of Watergate can be drastically altered, and even revolutionized, through allegiance to Jesus Christ.

Such is the ongoing story of Jeb Magruder. In reading it I think you will understand why I feel privileged to count him as a friend and a brother.

SENATOR MARK O. HATFIELD

12

Key Persons

Jack Anderson—Washington political columnist who opposed Nixon administration.

Gene Arnold—Ex-Marine Colonel, friend and Christian brother.

Jim (Doc) Benjamin—Doctor, prisoner at Allenwood.

Benny—Ex-cop and prisoner at Allenwood.

Richard Ben-Veniste—Lawyer. Prosecutor in Watergate case under special prosecutor.

Jim Bierbower—Lawyer. Heads law firm of Bierbower and Rockefeller. Retained as my counsel in April, 1973.

Bill Brehm—Friend and member of Covenant Group; former Assistant Secretary of Defense.

Jimmy Breslin—Author and columnist from New York.

Donner Buchet—Friend and Christian brother.

Donald Campbell—Lawyer. Assistant U.S. Attorney. Worked with Silbert and Glanzer on initial Watergate case.

Carl—Prisoner at Allenwood.

Doug Coe—Head of Fellowship House. Washington, D.C.

Charles Colson—Lawyer. Special Counsel to President Nixon. Prolifically involved in Watergate and related activities. Now a committed Christian and author of *Born Again*. Engaged in a prison ministry. Served a prison term.

Archibald Cox—Lawyer. First special prosecutor appointed by the President for the Watergate case.

Al Davis—Lawyer associated with Jim Bierbower. Entered the case as my attorney in the latter stages.

John Dean—Lawyer. Counsel to President Nixon, involved in initial planning of Watergate, turned prosecution witness, implicated Nixon in cover-up. Served a prison term.

Bill Edwards—Prisoner at Allenwood.

John Ehrlichman—Lawyer. Assistant to President Nixon for Domestic Affairs. Involved in Watergate cover-up. Now serving four-year sentence in Federal prison.

Colleen and Louis Evans, Jr.—Minister National Presbyterian Church, Washington, D.C. and his wife.

Cornelius Gallagher—Former Congressman from New Jersey. Prisoner at Allenwood.

Seymour Glanzer—Lawyer. Assistant U.S. attorney. Worked

with Silbert on initial Watergate case. Now in private practice.

H. R. Haldeman—Chief of Staff to President Nixon. Involved in cover-up of Watergate. Recently completed four-year sentence in Federal prison.

Mark Hatfield—Senator from Oregon, friend and Christian brother.

Larry Higby—H. R. Haldeman's original assistant known as the "gopher," which translated means go for this or that.

Harold Hughes—Former Senator from Iowa, involved with Doug Coe at Fellowship House.

E. Howard Hunt—Ex-CIA Agent. Original planner, with Liddy, of Watergate breakin. Served second longest prison term.

Leon Jaworski—Lawyer. Special prosecutor who replaced Archibald Cox after the Saturday Night Massacre in 1973.

Herbert Kalmbach—Lawyer. Fund-raiser for President Nixon. Involved in Watergate cover-up, turned prosecution witness. Served prison term.

Egil "Bud" Krogh—Lawyer. Special counsel to President Nixon, involved in Ellsberg case, turned prosecution witness. Served prison term.

Fred LaRue—Friend and advisor to John Mitchell. My closest friend at CRP. Involved in Watergate cover-up. Served prison term.

G. Gordon Liddy—Lawyer. Ex-FBI Agent. Original planner of Watergate breakin. Served longest prison term of any Watergate conspirator.

Clark MacGregor—Former Congressman from Minnesota. Became Director of CRP after Mitchell resigned in July, 1972.

Robert Mardian—Lawyer. Assistant Attorney General under President Nixon, later official at CRP. Involved in cover-up. Convicted in Watergate trial, conviction later overturned by Appeals Court.

James McCord—Former CIA Agent and Security Director at CRP. Part of the original Watergate Seven who were directly involved in the breakin. Served a prison term.

John Mitchell—Lawyer. Attorney General and Director of CRP until Watergate breakin June, 1972. Involved in planning of breakin and the cover-up. Now serving four-year sentence in Federal prison.

Bob Mitchell—President of Young Life and close friend.

James Neal—Lawyer. Senior assistant to the special prosecutor responsible for the prosecution of the Watergate case that involved Haldeman, Mitchell and Ehrlichman.

Paul Noe—Fraud expert. Prisoner at Holabird.

Larry O'Brien—Chairman of Democratic Party at the time of Watergate. Now President of National Basketball Association.

Tip O'Neill—Congressman from Massachusetts, now Speaker of the House of Representatives.

Kenneth Parkinson—Lawyer. Hired by CRP to defend against civil suits relating to Watergate. Implicated in Watergate prosecution. Indicted but exonerated by the jury.

Don Rumsfeld—Former Congressman. Assistant to President Nixon during Watergate. Later Secretary of Defense under President Ford.

Johnny Sample—Former National Football League star. Prisoner at Allenwood.

Jim Sharp—Lawyer. Also associated with Jim Bierbower and was specifically assigned as my attorney.

Bill Starr—Former president of Young Life responsible for hiring me.

Earl Silbert—Lawyer. Assistant U.S. attorney responsible for initial Watergate case. Now U.S. attorney for Washington, D.C.

Judge John Sirica—The original Watergate judge who continued to play a major role in most of the Watergate cases.

Skitch—Prisoner at Holabird.

Gordon Strachan—Lawyer. Initially my assistant in White House. Later Haldeman's political aide. Involved in planning and cover-up of Watergate breakin. Later indicted but case dismissed.

Lou Tonti—Former New Jersey State Highway Commissioner. Prisoner at Allenwood.

Bill Turnblazer—United Mine Worker official. Prisoner at Holabird.

Jill Vollner—Lawyer. Prosecutor in Watergate case under special prosecutor.

Chronology of Events

November 5, 1934	Born Staten Island, New York
June, 1952	Graduation from Curtis High School, Staten Island, New York
1952–1954	Freshman and Sophomore years at Williams College, Williamstown, Massachusetts
1954–1956	U.S. Army—Served in Korea
1956–1958	Final two years at Williams—graduated with B.A. in Political Science with honors
1958–1960	Sales representative for Crown Zellerbach Corporation, San Francisco, CA
1959	Married to Gail Barnes Nicholas in Los Angeles, CA
1960	Ward Chairman for Nixon-Lodge, Kansas City, MO
1960–1962	Consultant—Booz, Allen and Hamilton, Inc., Chicago, IL
1960	September 20: Birth of first child, Whitney Craig
1961–1963	Graduate School of Business, University of Chicago—graduated with M.B.A. in marketing
1962	October 19: Birth of second child, Justin Scott
1962	Area Chairman for Donald Rumsfeld in the 13th Congressional District, IL

1962–1966	Merchandise Manager for Jewel Tea Company, Chicago, IL
1964	Chairman for 13th Congressional District, Illinois, Goldwater-Miller organization
1964	May 9: Birth of third child, Tracy Lynn
1966	Campaign Manager for Governor Richard B. Ogilvie of Illinois in primary campaign for President of the Cook County Board
1966–1968	Merchandise Manager and Buyer for Broadway-Hale stores, Los Angeles, CA
1967	March 24: Birth of fourth child, Stuart Cameron
1967–1968	Southern California coordinator for the Nixon for President Committee
1968–1969	President and Chief Executive Officer of Consumer Developments, Inc. and Cosmetics Industry, Inc., Los Angeles, CA
1969–1973	White House years:
1969–1971	Special Assistant to the President and Deputy Director of Communications for Executive Branch
1971–1972	Deputy Campaign Director of the Committee to Reelect the President
1972	June 17: Watergate Breakin

1972–1973	Executive Director of the Inaugural Committee
1973	Commerce Department, Director of Policy
1973	June 19: Senate Watergate public hearings
1973–1974	Consultant, Metropolitan Research Services, Washington, D.C.
1974–1975	Federal prison at Allenwood, PA, and Ft. Holabird, MD
1975–Present	Director of Communications Young Life Campaign, Colorado Springs, CO
1976–Present	Pursuing a Master's degree in Divinity, Institute of Youth Ministries of Fuller Theological Seminary/Young Life
1978	Enrolling at Princeton Seminary to pursue a Master's degree in Divinity and in Social Work

From Power to Peace

His wife, Gail, described Jeb after his prison experience as "a different man. He is more sensitive to our needs and more appreciative of our strengths." (From *A Gift of Love*) *Paul Rey photo*

1

My Double Life

I SLID INTO THE BOOTH opposite Gail and almost immediately a waitress handed us menus. There were only a few other customers in the restaurant.

A moment later, the waitress was back. "Can I take your order?" she asked. Ordinarily I might have needed a little more time to make up my mind, but not today.

"I'd like a steak," I said, not even looking at the menu. "A nice big sirloin."

"You don't have to order a big steak," she said. "We have a small luncheon steak, if you'd rather have that." She reached over and pointed to a white card stapled to the menu.

"Thanks, but I really want a *big* steak—the biggest one you've got," I answered. I had the feeling this was going to be the last good piece of meat I'd have for a long time.

Gail ordered a salad. She wasn't hungry.

The steak was delicious and I ate every bit of it. Neither Gail nor I said a word. I think we both had the strange feeling that if we started a conversation, there wouldn't be enough time to finish it.

I looked at my watch and saw it was almost 2 P.M.

"Time to go?" Gail asked.

"Yes," I said, signaling the waitress for the bill.

Outside it was sunny and warm. The Pennsylvania hills are beautiful in June, and everywhere you look the hills are thick with large old trees in full bloom, and the air sparkles in the sunshine. On this day, especially, I was grateful for the good weather.

Allenwood was only a few miles north along Route 15, and unless you needed gas or were going to prison, you would have no reason to stop there. We pulled into the gas station and I drank a Coke while the attendant filled the tank. Gail would be going home alone, and it was a long distance between gas stations.

The prison was another five miles north in the town of Montgomery (why it was called Allenwood, I don't know). When we came to a sign, FEDERAL PRISON CAMP, we turned left off Route 15, and after one more mile, we were there.

They were waiting for us—reporters, photographers, and TV cameramen. As soon as our car slowed down at the gate they rushed toward us. Flashbulbs went off, cameras began to grind, and reporters with pencils, pads, and cassette recorders pushed against each other, asking their questions all at once. I felt Gail flinch at my side and I knew what she was thinking—Was there no privacy, *even now*?

The prison gate was open and we could have kept the car moving until we were inside. But they would have waited for Gail to come out, and I didn't want that. I squeezed Gail's hand hard. "Honey, I think I'd better get out and talk to them a few minutes. It'll be better that way."

She shook her head angrily.

"It will be, honey," I insisted. "Just for a couple of minutes."

When I opened the door, the crowd dropped back to let me out, and then they came at me again, shouting questions and grinding film. Lights were exploding from all angles.

I knew several of the men and women. They had been keeping me company for the past two years, ever since the Watergate story broke.

"Hey, Jeb, how does it feel to be going to prison?"

"Are you looking forward to it, Jeb?"

"What are you going to do with all that time, Jeb?"

"It's a long way from Washington, huh, Jeb?"

I had to agree with whoever said it was a long way from Washington. Not so much in terms of miles, perhaps, but in what had happened to me between then and now.

I couldn't say much. How I was going to react to being in prison, I had no idea. I blinked at the lights moving closer and closer to my face as the cameramen moved in for a good look at a man who was about to lose his freedom.

Was it only two years ago that I had been on top of the world? And that a reporter hanging on my words and a flashbulb momentarily blinding me meant I really had it made?

All my life I'd gone to church. I enjoyed the services, especially if the minister was a strong preacher. I liked the atmosphere of the church itself and believed it was good for people to come together and worship God. It seemed like the right thing to do, and I wanted to be part of it.

To me, a minister—especially an effective one—represented the kind of person everyone ought to be. *And wouldn't it be nice,* I used to ask myself, *if we all could be that way?*—knowing very well that such a thing never could happen. Ministers weren't like other men. They were sheltered from the real world and didn't have to make compromises. Still, it was pleasant to listen to a sermon about the kind of life a Christian ought to live. We all knew it could only happen in church, and that the other six days of the week—in fact, even the rest of Sunday—we lived by different rules.

The same was true of God and Jesus Christ. I believed in the things they stood for, and I enjoyed reading about them in the Bible, but I was convinced they were obsolete for my lifetime. I loved God, but he seemed far away, with his head literally in the clouds and no idea of what was really going on down here on earth. It was just as well, I thought —he wouldn't have been comfortable with the way we do things down here.

For instance, I knew he wouldn't have approved of the double life I was leading early in 1973. I had been living that way for six months, ever since the day after the June Watergate breakin. But by Richard Nixon's second inauguration, the contrast between what I believed and how I functioned was especially ironic.

I had been spending much of my time covering up the involvement of the White House and Committee to Reelect the President (CRP) in the breakin. Almost every day I had met with or spoken to John Dean, John Mitchell, Bob Mardian, Gordon Strachan, and Fred LaRue, working out the cover-up story in minute detail. Twice, in August and September of 1972, I had appeared before a grand jury investigating the breakin, and, under oath, had perjured myself. I insisted that I, as Deputy Director of the Committee to Reelect the President, and others on my staff knew nothing of the attempt to burglarize the Democratic Party headquarters. I claimed it was a scheme G. Gordon Liddy and E. Howard Hunt had concocted on their own—foolishly, overzealously, perhaps, but absolutely without our knowledge or authorization.

My testimony had been accepted by the prosecutors—Earl Silbert, Seymour Glanzer, and Donald Campbell—and by the grand jury. I had every reason to believe that the Watergate furor would eventually die down. Later in January 1973, after the Inauguration, I would have to testify again at the trial of Liddy and Hunt and the other men who committed the actual breakin, but I didn't see why that shouldn't go as smoothly as my other two appearances in court. I had told myself the cover-up story so often that it seemed more real than the truth.

The lying was one of the worst things that was happening to me then, although I didn't realize it. Actually, neither I nor the others involved in the cover-up called it lying, and none of us seemed to be bothered by it. We were more concerned about our cause—the reelection and second administration of Richard Nixon—and if we had to conceal the truth to protect that cause, so be it. I suppose there was some comfort in the knowledge that we were in this together and could trust each other.

Unfortunately, if you want a lie to work, you have

to tell the same story to everybody, with no exceptions. What I told to the grand jury and the prosecutors I also told to my staff, to my friends, to the press, and even to my wife and children. I couldn't risk a slip of the tongue, not when I was under oath. But I did make one exception. I *had* to level with someone, perhaps just to hold on to a thread of reality. I couldn't tell my family the truth because I didn't want to pass the burden of concealment on to them. And anyone else might have leaked the information to the press. So I talked to Fred LaRue, who not only worked closely with me, but was a good friend. Since he was involved as well, I knew he wouldn't tell anyone else.

I was putting in long hours in those days, but even after my work was done I often lingered at the office, talking things over with Fred, the two of us drinking Scotch and trying to second-guess how the cover-up was going. It felt good to let my guard down. When we could see that the cover-up was going well, I felt even better. Apparently it would not influence the '72 election. And it didn't.

The cover-up was just one part of me, however. The other side was totally different—under pressure, but out in the open. Rather than trying to keep the public eye off the President, my job was to attract attention to him and help get him reelected to office. I loved every minute of it.

Earlier in my life if anyone had ever asked me what would be the most exciting job in the world, I would have answered, "Running a Presidential election campaign." I never really expected to have such an opportunity. But now it was happening. I was running Nixon's campaign. John Mitchell was head of CRP until July, when he resigned and was replaced by Clark MacGregor; however, as is customary with committee heads, it is their personal luster rather than their time which they are called upon to give to the job. As the number two man, putting in full time and all the overtime necessary, I was responsible for working out the details of the campaign.

Richard Nixon won the 1972 election by a landslide, and his campaign was called the most effective, most efficiently run in history. I was proud of my part in it. Strangely enough, though I had reached a peak in my career, I was very apprehensive about some of the steps I had taken to get there. That's when I finally understood what it meant to be "caught on the horns of a dilemma," although I tried not to think about it in those terms.

As an acknowledgment of my part in the campaign, I was appointed Executive Director of the Inaugural Committee, second only to J. Willard Marriott, the Chairman. I had a full-time staff of 400 and an additional 4000 volunteers. It was a prestigious job—not that it was easy, which it certainly wasn't, but it implied tremendous power.

The Inauguration itself, the actual swearing in of the President, was administered traditionally by the Senate, but the other ceremonies during the three-day period were arranged by the Inaugural Committee. These included about ten major events to be held in various parts of the city, with performances by some of the most outstanding entertainers and artists in the country. Much to the distress of the Washington Symphony, the Philadelphia Symphony Orchestra under Eugene Ormandy, which was the President's favorite, was invited to perform at the Kennedy Center on the evening before the swearing-in ceremonies. The concert was to be followed by a formal dinner for the favored few in typically elegant Washington style. Also during the Inaugural there were to be other concerts featuring

Frank Sinatra, Bob Hope, Johnny Cash, and other celebrities. After the swearing-in, there would be a parade with all fifty states participating, and at night there would be several formal balls. The final event was to be a White House worship service the morning after the Inauguration, setting the proper note of seriousness and almost holy intent for the coming four years.

The seating capacity at each event was anywhere from 500 to 250,000 people, which seems reasonable until you consider that *everyone* wanted tickets to everything and there simply weren't enough to go around. To some people, just getting a ticket was a big deal in itself, the ultimate payoff, but to many others the critical issue was *where* they were to sit. Everyone wanted to sit next to the President (or as near as a person's influence could bring him), and it was no easy task to allocate seats among senators, congressmen, government and state officials, and party fat cats without insulting someone's ego. Deciding where Ronald Reagan and Nelson Rockefeller would sit in relation to the President and to each other was a delicate matter that couldn't very well be left to subordinates, so that and other touchy decisions were left to me. I also allocated limousines to the VIP's—and without a limousine, you just weren't a VIP.

For a few weeks before the Inauguration, I was everybody's friend. Some of the most important people in the country treated me like a brother and I saw nothing but smiles on their faces. I was receiving a great deal of publicity, and the *Washington Post* ran a feature article about our family on the front page of the Style section of the Sunday issue. I began to see myself as others were seeing me: a young man on his way up in the political world. In short, I had many of the things people wanted, and in a city like Washington, where protocol is synonymous with power, that made me King Kong in a three-piece suit.

The ceremonies went beautifully, drawing the largest attendance in Inauguration history. Most of the events began and ended on time. Even the parade was on schedule, and it was notorious for lasting so long that a newly elected President usually began his administration with a cold caught while standing outside on a raw winter day for as long as four hours. Scheduled to last two hours, the parade traditionally runs overtime because the various units get farther and farther apart as they march down Pennsylvania Avenue. Our staff solved that problem by sending parade marshals along to keep everyone moving briskly, and so we were able to hold the viewing time down to exactly two hours. The President appreciated that.

The last time I saw Richard Nixon was the morning after his second inauguration as President of the United States. We met at the White House worship service which ended the ceremonies.

I was familiar with these so-called church services because the ideas for them came up in staff meetings when I was Special Assistant to the President during Richard Nixon's first administration. They never were intended to be spiritual, but rather political in tone. And they served as a convenient way to invite certain kinds of people to the White House—the kind who just didn't seem to fit into other occasions—and earn their good will. The services were nonsectarian and began with an unmemorable prayer and a few hymns. The sermon might be delivered by a rabbi, a priest, or a minister, and it always seemed more like a semi-political speech in support of the President. Then after the service the guests were invited to an excellent buffet. Frankly, if you weren't seeking spiritual nourishment, you could have had a wonderful time there.

I had attended about three of these services and didn't care for them, although I recognized their political value. Ordinarily I avoided them, but the morning after the Inauguration was something special and I was there. The President, usually a somber man, looked happy and rested, almost jubilant. He came over to me, shook my hand, and smiled as he said, "Jeb, I've been to five Inaugurals, and this was the best one of them all. I'm sure it's the finest in the history of our country."

I had worked for this man for a long time, even before he was in office. I admired and respected him almost to the point of reverence, and believed in the goals he had set for himself, his staff, and the country. So his remarks were the highest compliment I had ever received. I remember the sense of relief that flowed through me then. I had been tired—the pressure of the past several months had been exhausting. But all of a sudden it made sense. The endless planning and replanning, the checking and follow-through of thousands of details, the long hours on the job coordinating extremely sensitive elements of events that would become part of our history, the time spent away from home and family, the anxiety of watching a magnificently complex program unfold without any of the mishaps that easily could have happened—it was worth the tension, the strained family relationships and the tranquilizers. The President was pleased.

As his hand released mine, even the schizophrenic life I had been leading seemed justified. But, then, he didn't know the details about that. Or so I thought.

The decisiveness of the 1972 election gave Richard Nixon the mandate he had wanted for so long. As far back as 1969, when I first began to work for him, he was thinking not only about his first four years in office, but the next four years as well. In many of our staff meetings, Haldeman made it clear that it would take the President more than four years to build up the kind of power he would need to get his programs through a Democratic-controlled Congress.

To me, that kind of a goal didn't seem unnatural for a newly elected President, and I imagine it's the kind of dream shared by every President in one way or another. Nor did it seem to conflict with the democratic process of our government, because if a President did a good job for four years, most likely the voters would reelect him.

But after a while it became evident that Nixon wanted more than a second term in office. Some historians think he aimed at a third, which would have involved a constitutional amendment, but I don't believe he ever thought about that seriously. Actually, from his perspective, a third term would have been unnecessary. He intended to control the Executive Branch of the government by establishing "a perpetual Presidency." He was so convinced that his kind of administration was better for the country than anything the Democrats could offer, that he wanted to be able to pick his successors. That meant two things: a Republican candidate had to be able to win elections—we had just proved that could be done; and he had to be able to destroy any opposition candidates—we were well on our way to doing that.

In 1968 most of the government department heads were replaced with Republicans, not all of them loyal to Richard Nixon. During his second term Nixon planned to gain control of the Federal bureaucracy by replacing the heads of departments with his own people. Eventually he would be able to call upon agencies such as the FBI, the CIA, the FTC, the FCC, the IRS, and others to provide him with any information that would damage the image of a potential political rival. (I remember how overjoyed he was when he heard the news about Chappaquiddick. Afterward, not satisfied with the data from routine investigations of that unhappy event, he sent E. Howard Hunt to Chappaquiddick to dig up whatever he could. If Senator Edward Kennedy ever decided to run against Nixon—or perhaps against Nixon's eventual successor—Nixon wanted to be ready to finish him off before he got started.)

Government agencies would come in handy in other ways. Sometimes the mere mention of one in a news story—leaked deliberately, of course—would be enough to hurt another candidate. For instance, if it became known that the IRS was about to examine a candidate's income tax returns, that in itself would cast suspicion on his honesty, regardless of the propriety of the returns. Then there were ways in which the agencies could be used to harass people —political rivals, critics of the administration, or targets of a presidential grudge. The IRS, as I learned much later, can make life so miserable for a person that he finds it almost impossible to do anything other than search for the material "proof" they endlessly require. And even someone as formidable as *Washington Post* publisher Katherine Graham could be hounded by the Federal Communications Commission. Add to these methods the disclosure of skeletons, however minor or ancient, in so many political closets, and you have an awesome arsenal of weapons to shoot down future presidential hopefuls. Nixon could thereby eliminate the more attractive Democrats before they even became candidates, leaving the least effective ones to run against Republicans of his choice. (As far as 1976 was concerned, I always thought Nixon would have chosen John Connally to succeed him.)

To do it all, the President had to be able to count on the loyalty of those he appointed to key government positions. In typical Nixonian fashion, his definition of loyalty was extreme. Anyone who was with him *unquestioningly* was on his side, but anyone who received any of his views with even the mildest criticism was out. Consequently, after the 1972 election, there was a quiet, bloodless purge in the Administration. And that was unfortunate, because many of those released were actually devoted to the President. They simply didn't think he was infallible, and they let him know it.

For example, "Pete" Peterson, then Secretary of Commerce, had been one of the most forceful and effective members of the Cabinet. But because Pete and his wife attended Georgetown parties, hosted by the "liberals" in town, or "the enemy," he was considered disloyal on the basis of "guilt by association," and was fired by the President at the urging of several key White House aides.

Of course, at the time I didn't have that problem. I loved the man. And I was not alone.

That's why it struck me as rather odd when, late in January, shortly after I had perjured myself again at the trial of Liddy, Hunt, and the Watergate burglars, John Mitchell said to me, "Jeb, maybe you ought to go back into business."

We were having lunch together in New York, and he had just complimented me on my performance in three government-related jobs. I thought I had made it pretty clear to him and everyone else that I wanted to stay in the government. If I had done so well there, why should I get out?

When I questioned Mitchell about his comment he said something to the effect that I could make a lot more money in business than I could in government.

"I've always known that," I said. I had taken a $10,000 cut in income to join the White House staff in 1969. I had been president of my own companies and before that I had held numerous management positions with large corporations. "But I still like being in government," I added.

"Why don't you try running for office?" Mitchell suggested. "Take a trip out to California. Talk to some of our people there. Look over the situation."

That wasn't exactly what I had in mind by "being in government," but I followed his advice, at least up to a point. I sized up the situation in my home state of California and decided that I didn't want to run for office. Maybe sometime in the future, but not then. There were great plans for the second Nixon Administration and I wanted to be in on them.

I didn't know until much later that I had become a threat to the White House staff. As far as I could tell, Watergate appeared to be dying a natural death, but they had a different way of looking at things. I had stuck to my cover-up story as had several others associated with me; the Wright Patman committee investigating the money found in possession of the Watergate burglars had been effectively stopped by a committee vote. But the Ervin committee was beginning to form and no one knew what we could expect from that investigation. The grand jury might also reconvene.

Would I—and would others—continue to protect

higher-ups involved in the cover-up, or would we implicate them when the pressure was on? The staff decided to play it safe, in one way or another. If the cover-up broke down under questioning, they would blame the breakin on me. If it held up, it was better for them if I just faded from the scene. Consequently their advice to me was to go "back into business."

Based upon my previous performances, I was eligible for any number of interesting government jobs, but almost all of them would have required senatorial approval. Ordinarily that would have been a routine matter, but now it was a sensitive situation. Under questioning by members of the Senate I might reveal something that would reopen Watergate. L. Patrick Gray had already done that when he came up for Senate approval of his appointment as head of the FBI.

Not knowing what was happening behind the scenes, I was confused and disappointed by the snag in my career. Only a short time ago there was nowhere to go but up. I was not only Haldeman's man, but Mitchell's as well, and I couldn't have asked for better recommendations. But all of a sudden these same men seemed to be telling me—although not in so many words—to go on my way and in another direction.

Then I started getting strange phone calls from Larry Higby, Haldeman's aide, from Haldeman himself, and from John Dean. I say "strange" because the calls took on a pattern. Higby, Haldeman, or Dean would ask me questions about the meetings and discussions leading up to the Watergate breakin. Knowing that we were in on it together, I was open about my answers. My callers seemed to want their memories refreshed, and I obliged them. I would go over the whole Watergate breakin plan in detail while my caller kept saying he just couldn't remember such a meeting or such a conversation or such a decision. Much later I learned that these phone calls were taped on the other end and that the questions were designed to make it appear that I had proceeded with the breakin on my own.

Each caller came off on the tape as being surprised that such a thing could have happened. "I don't recall any such plans being discussed," was their attitude, at which point I would recite the entire Watergate story all over again.

I wasn't entirely naive. Although I didn't realize my conversations were being taped, I sensed that I was being set up as a scapegoat in reserve. It hurt, but I can't say it came as a shock. As much as I wanted to believe that my friends wouldn't let me down, intuitively I realized that if it came down to a choice between them or me taking the blame, I would be chosen. I knew them and I knew the system. I sensed that they planned to set me up, and there didn't seem to be anything I could do about it.

Meanwhile, something else began to happen inside me. In the early days of the cover-up there had been a sense of camaraderie among Haldeman, Dean, Mardian, Mitchell, Strachan, LaRue, and me. Our first reaction to Liddy's bungled breakin had been: "How did we ever turn a nut like that loose?" Then we moved on to asking, "How can we get this thing under wraps?" It became a game: Would the FBI get us or could we outwit the FBI? When Liddy, Hunt, McCord, and the others agreed to take the blame, we were pretty confident of the outcome.

Our loyalty was to the President, and we agreed on the rationalizations we used among ourselves to suppress whatever sense of wrongdoing we might have felt. I don't think any one of us believed, deep down, that he was acting in behalf of national security; but it was an impressive, comforting banner to salute.

On August 16, 1972, as I finished my first sworn testimony before the grand jury, I felt the first twinge of uneasiness. I was no longer telling the story of a crime; I was involved in the crime itself. I had the feeling that Earl Silbert, the prosecutor, wasn't buying my entire story that Liddy and Hunt had acted on their own, but he didn't have the kind of evidence he needed to dispute me. Besides, he was a practical man—he wanted Liddy and Hunt, and he knew I could deliver them to him.

Even then I had a few doubts about the continued support of the others involved in the cover-up—I could see that some maneuvering was going on. Chuck Colson was staying as far away from the whole affair as he could, and Dean was saying, much too often, "Don't worry, Jeb, everything'll be all right. We'll protect you." I hadn't asked for such assurances and it made me uncomfortable to get so many of them. Besides, no one was offering anything specific.

I allowed none of these misgivings to come to the surface, but they began to affect my behavior nonetheless. One day in July of '72 Larry Higby called me and said that Bob Haldeman wanted McGovern's schedule.

"No problem," I said. "We can get it through the normal press channels two or three days in advance."

"Not good enough," he said. "We need it further in advance."

"There's no way we can do that," I told him.

"Yes, there is," he replied. "You can put a guy in his headquarters."

"Wait a minute!" I almost yelled. "We're in the

middle of a criminal case already. I'm not going to put anyone in McGovern's headquarters."

Higby let it go at that, but later Haldeman called me about the same thing. Again I refused, and Haldeman was furious with me. Obviously, he was operating on the principle of "business as usual," whereas I was beginning to think business wasn't "as usual."

After the Inaugural, with our goal accomplished and our cause protected, the cover-up group was scattered and the sense of camaraderie dissipated. Each one of us had to look back at things in his own way and from his own perspective, and that made a difference. There simply weren't enough hands left to hoist the banner of national security, and as far as I was concerned, that excuse was a failure. I began to realize how wrong the breakin itself had been—and the cover-up was a much worse breach of public trust. There was no longer any way I could justify it in my own mind.

Naturally I wasn't about to turn myself in to the prosecutors. Like everyone else involved, I was hoping Watergate would go away and never come back. But, having admitted a portion of reality to myself, I knew I could not tell the cover-up story again under oath. I was becoming aware that I could be indicted and sent to prison for what I had done, and I accepted that possibility. With luck, though, I thought I would be able to avoid such a crisis.

I say "luck" because I saw too many possibilities for the crisis to actually occur. John Dean had cautioned me about Earl Silbert—"Watch out for him, he's a fox," he had said—and he was right. I had the feeling, as I went over my trial testimony with Silbert, that he was not going to be satisfied with the conviction of the seven burglars. If he were given the slightest additional bit of evidence, I felt that he would not hesitate to reconvene the grand jury and begin another investigation.

We also had reason to be concerned about one of the seven. Jim McCord, the former White House security guard, was said to be having second thoughts about taking so much of the blame on himself. I wasn't consoled by the fact that McCord had no direct knowledge about the others involved in the cover-up. Suppose he had heard some names mentioned? Even second-hand information would be enough to get the questioning started all over again.

Yes, luck was what I needed.

Finally my message seemed to be getting through. Haldeman and Dean found a job for me—a Level Four position as Director of Policy in the Department of Commerce. Usually a Level Four job required Senate confirmation, but this was one of the few that didn't. After Haldeman assured Fred Dent, Secretary of Commerce, that there was absolutely no truth to the rumors that I was involved in Watergate, I got the job.

Getting into the new job eased some of my anxieties. Working with economists and laying out administrative policy was the kind of thing I was accustomed to doing and I enjoyed it. Unfortunately, it wasn't going to last long.

Many people erroneously believe that the Watergate cover-up was blown by *Washington Post* reporters Bob Woodward and Carl Bernstein. Actually they were minor figures in the events and were not even on the scene at the time the cover-up began to fall apart. One of the real heroes—if there needs to be a hero—was Judge John Sirica who presided at the trial of the Watergate burglars. Liddy, Hunt, McCord, and the others had been convicted late in January '73 and were to be sentenced in March. Judge Sirica let it be known that he planned to give them the stiffest sentences possible. Obviously, he wasn't convinced they were telling the truth and hoped that the prospect of long prison terms might break them down. In the case of McCord, he was right. Shortly before the date set for sentencing, McCord sent a letter to Sirica, expressing his willingness to implicate higher-ups involved in the conspiracy.

As soon as we heard about the letter, Fred LaRue and I knew the cover-up was coming apart in so many places it could never be put back together. Not everyone agreed with us. Mitchell thought he could stay out of it and Haldeman thought it was "a public relations problem." I could understand why they felt that way. They hadn't been called to testify over and over again, as LaRue and I had been. They were farther removed from the investigations, while we were right in the middle of them.

We could see the holes in the cover-up story as they appeared, and when those holes began to grow bigger we couldn't ignore the probable result. As had happened so many times to people in the White House, Nixon and Haldeman were cut off from what was really happening in the world outside. They had forgotten, as they flew above the crowded streets in their helicopters or slid through intersections in White House limousines, that other people who ran through red lights were getting tickets. Or worse than that, being arrested.

The Magruder home in Colorado Springs.
Paul Rey photo

Jeb and Jean Ryan, his administrative assistant at Young Life.

Jeb acted as a consultant to other departments at the Young Life headquarters. Here he is with Harry MacDonald, International Coordinator, who started the international ministry in Brazil in 1963.

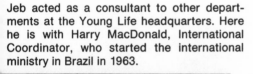

Jeb and Bob Mitchell, President of Young Life, have become close friends.

Paul Rey photos

Jeb and friend at a Young Life weekend in Colorado Springs.

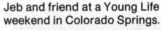

Whitney, now 17, was old enough to comprehend the Watergate affair.

Justin is the artist of the family.

Tracy, 13, is Gail's assistant "homemaker," scholar, and athlete.

Stuart is the youngest, and felt an acute sense of loss while Jeb was away. It was his birthday party Jeb was able to attend while still in prison.

Gail at work in the family kitchen. *Paul Rey photos*

Jeb at a meditative moment. *Paul Rey photo*

2

Don't Tell the Truth

MANY THINGS WENT through my mind after McCord broke down.

Until then, I considered a crime to be an act of violence against another person—a rape, a murder, an assault, or a robbery. I knew that what I had done was unethical, in some areas illegal, but like most white-collar lawbreakers, I felt that I was acting against something or someone faceless. "They" were out to get us, so we made sure they didn't, or at least we tried. My rationalization was: since I didn't consider myself a criminal, how could I commit a crime?

But late in March of '73 I had to face the fact that I had broken the law just as surely as if I had gone out in the street and mugged someone. I had to deal with the inevitability of disclosure, conviction, and probably a prison sentence.

I can't describe the guilt that came over me when I saw what that would do to my family. Besides the shock and the shame they would experience, how would they get along financially if I went to prison? And what kind of sentence could I expect to get?

Around that same time Robert Vesco (the New Jersey financier indicted for illegal campaign contributions) solved his problems by running off to Costa Rica, a nation which does not exercise its extradition rights. That gave me an idea. I was still free—maybe I could get out of the country. So one day I called a friend in the State Department.

"We need a little information for some legislation we're thinking about over here," I said, hoping it sounded like a casual inquiry for the Department. "The Secretary would like a list of any countries which do not have extradition treaties with us—can you get that for me?"

"Sure," he replied. "No trouble."

While I waited for the list, I had all our passports updated—mine, Gail's, the kids—supposedly for a trip to a World Trade Fair in Paris in behalf of the Commerce Department. Something told me I would never make the fair.

When I received the list from the State Department, I felt sick. Extradition treaties are very complicated, and in some countries a person can be extradited for some crimes and not for others. In only a few instances were there no treaties at all and they weren't the kind of countries where I could have found a job. Since I didn't have Vesco's millions, they were out of the question. Besides, as I sat in my office, reading and rereading the list, I remembered something a lawyer friend had once said to me about people who left the country to avoid prosecution: "It doesn't work. Sooner or later they can't live with themselves and they have to come back."

Suicide was another possibility I thought about, but not for long. A congressman from Maryland, who had been implicated in the laundering of campaign funds, chose that way out of his predicament. But I couldn't do it. Suicide required something, perhaps a kind of despair that I just didn't have.

I knew I didn't have much time left before the investigation would close in on me again. Not wanting to involve anyone else if I could possibly avoid it, I spent many hours with Fred LaRue, exploring ways we could protect the others, especially the President. I was sure, by then, that the President himself was involved in the cover-up. It was not like Haldeman to do something that big on his own initiative; he was a man who carried out orders and he had only one superior.

By that time Dean and I were on the front pages of the newspapers almost every day, and as far as I was concerned the cover-up had already come apart. There would be another inquiry, perhaps more than one. What I needed right away was legal advice. And John Mitchell agreed with me, although he would handle his own problems in a different manner. He even recommended a lawyer, James Bierbower.

"But don't tell your lawyer the truth," Mitchell said matter-of-factly. "Tell him the cover-up story." Assuming that he knew best, that's what I decided to do.

I told the cover-up story to Jim Bierbower, and then I repeated it to his associate, Jim Sharp. Bierbower was not a specialist in criminal law, but Sharp was. Before joining Bierbower's firm, Sharp had been one of the most successful prosecutors on the U.S. Attorney's staff. He had had an unusual opportunity to gain experience in criminal cases because at that time the District of Columbia had no prosecutors of its own and relied on the U.S. attorneys to try its cases.

Sharp was a tall, slim young man in his late twenties, and I guessed that probably when he was younger he might have looked a little hippy-ish. Now his thick, black, curly hair was well trimmed, though his handlebar mustache was less than conservative. I liked him, but he worried me. He had me go over my story several times, sometimes in his office, sometimes in mine. One day in my office, after listening patiently to the now-familiar details, he leaned forward and looked me straight in the eye. "Jeb," he said, "pretty soon you're going to have to tell me the truth." He spoke quietly, but I felt as if a great big gong had gone off in my head. *He knows!* I had suspected it since the first day I had talked to him. He had too much experience with liars to be fooled by even the best of them.

I tried to bluff. "What do you mean? " I asked, forcing myself to smile, but not succeeding very well. The muscles in my jaw were too tight.

He shook his head and smiled at me a little sadly, "Just what I said." He got up to leave. "I hope you won't wait too long."

I didn't. The next day I called Sharp. "Jim, I'd like to come over right now," I said. "I want to talk to you."

That afternoon, as I sat in his office and told him what really happened, I saw the expression in his eyes change from intense interest to near-shock as the names came out: Mitchell, Haldeman, Dean, Ehrlichman, LaRue, Mardian, Strachan, and, by implication, the President.

"Jeb, this is going to bring down the whole government!" he said. Obviously he had suspected a more contained, lower-echelon conspiracy.

After Jim Bierbower heard my story, he and Sharp spelled out my alternatives. "You can stay with the cover-up story, if you want to," Bierbower said, "but if you do, you'll have to get another lawyer and try to stonewall him the way Mitchell will. Now that we know what the truth is, we can't be a party to perjury.

"Or, you can go to the prosecutors and tell them what you know. Maybe we can bargain for immunity."

There wasn't any question in my mind. I had to go to the prosecutors. My lawyers agreed that that was the best thing to do. "But I don't want immunity," I told them. The lying was over. I was experiencing the relief of telling the truth at last, and I couldn't stand the thought of negotiating about it. I wasn't seeing things very clearly, yet somehow I realized that my self-respect, or whatever was left of it, was at stake. For a while I may have lost the ability to distinguish between right and wrong, but I still knew that there were such things—and it was right that I should pay a penalty for what I had done. I had to go to prison. It was right for me and right for my family's evaluation of me, in spite of the hardships it would mean for all of us.

I was hoping, of course, that I would not receive a long prison sentence. Two days later, after my lawyers and I had spoken to the prosecutors and outlined what I had to say, it was agreed that I would be indicted on one felony count of obstruction of justice, which meant a maximum of five years in prison. I thought that was fair, considering that the actual sentence probably would be quite lenient for a first offender in a nonviolent crime.

Judge Sirica could have sentenced me right then

and there, but he didn't. I think he wanted to see the rest of the Watergate affair unfold, and besides, the prosecutors wanted to spend some time with me. It was more convenient for everyone if I didn't go directly to prison. So I was released under my own recognizance for a period that was to last fourteen months. It was a strange time in my life, both a blessing and a strain.

My first concern was how I was going to make a living for my family and also earn enough to help them through the time I would be in prison. I hated to think that Gail might have to take on a full–time job just when our children would need her more than ever. And the possibility that I might have to sit around with nothing to do but think about the mess I was in was more than I could take. Besides needing something to keep my mind busy, I had been brought up to believe that there was something wrong with a person who didn't work.

What a difference three months had made in my life. In January I had been ready for a high–level job in government or business. It became obvious by mid-April that either I would have to resign from the Commerce Department, or Secretary Fred Dent would have to fire me. After talking with him, we agreed that I would have to resign to spare the Department further embarrassment.

If anyone had a right to feel betrayed by me it was Fred Dent. After all, I had told him the cover-up story when he interviewed me and he had accepted Haldeman's assurances that I was not involved in any wrongdoing. But when I left the Department, he said, "Jeb, I can't fathom what happened, but I'm not going to sit here and be your judge. Things are going to be hard for you, but you seem to have made some peace with yourself—so I wish you the best of luck." I didn't know Fred Dent very well, but I'll never forget his kindness.

It was not so with most of the other people I knew. Before the Inaugural our telephone rang constantly and everywhere I went I was greeted as a friend. Now the phone was silent, except for an occasional crank call and press calls. The persistence of the reporters forced us to get an unlisted number and change it twice during the next two months. Many of the people I had known in the Administration behaved as if they had never heard of me. Yet I understood, and if I had been in their shoes I might have acted the same way. I was not good company, not if you were worried about your reputation in a town where reputation counted heavily. When I thought back over the friends I had lost, I realized that they hadn't been my friends at all. Nor had I been a friend to them. It had simply been advantageous for us to know each other because we could do something for each other. They had used me and I had used them, and now I was of no use to anyone.

There were some other meaningful relationships that it hurt to lose. One was my friendship with Don Rumsfeld. I had worked on his first election campaign in 1962 and on the night of his victory he had singled me out as "one of the most effective workers on his staff." We had known each other and, I think, liked each other for years, yet I never heard a word from him after I went to the prosecutors.

Needless to say, I heard nothing from Richard Nixon, but then, I didn't expect to.

I had never given much thought to the meaning of friendship. People liked each other or they didn't, and usually for good reasons. Generally I was easy to get along with, so I was accustomed to being liked. I reciprocated with other people who were pleasant and agreeable. But once I was near the top of the list of the Most Despised Persons in America, I thought that was a good enough reason for anyone to avoid me. Yet some people didn't. Some stayed on and didn't seem to care what anyone thought about them for remaining my friends. That was something new to me. I had nothing to exchange with them and still they gave me their friendship, in larger amounts than ever before. It didn't seem to matter what I had done. They loved me and Gail and the kids, and they weren't threatened by our notoriety. I used to wonder why.

Gilly and Joan Gillespie, who lived across the street, were wonderful. When our house was besieged by reporters, photographers, and TV cameramen, the Gillespies used to let me hide in their house until the street was clear. Rob Odle, who worked with me in the White House, still kept in touch. So did Bob Morgan who worked with me at CRP. He and I are still working together on other projects.

Much later I realized that these friends—these true friends—had an inner sense of security that had nothing to do with an image or the company they kept. They knew who they were and realized that the world did not revolve around them. All of them were aware of a higher being and many were committed Christians. I didn't know it then, but some were to become my teachers, for I had much to learn.

Since I didn't know how long I would be a free man I couldn't even attempt to get a job. But I was able to work as a consultant to several clients who were willing to use my services on a temporary basis. That was enough to keep me busy and ease some of my anxiety about money. But, in addition to the finances I needed to support my family during my imprisonment, there would be, of course, large legal fees.

The roles of Earl Silbert, Seymour Glanzer, and Donald Campbell, the original Watergate prosecutors, have been misunderstood and underrated. Too often they are blamed for accepting the cover-up story in the beginning—when actually there were no hard facts to dispute it—and rarely are they credited with putting together the evidence that made the Watergate convictions possible. These men were tough, experienced lawyers, but they also were compassionate, reasonable human beings. I didn't expect Earl Silbert to be overjoyed about the fact that I had lied to him before, but at least he didn't take it personally. Neither he nor the others were out for vengeance, and once I agreed to cooperate they took my word for it and we got down to work. As much as they were willing to have me make amends for the past, they did not let that conflict with their determination to get at the truth in all its details. They ended my hope that I would not have to involve anyone besides myself. Whatever I knew about Watergate had to come out.

Earl Silbert wanted me to take a lie detector test. As he put it to my lawyers, "Look, we think Jeb is telling the truth now, but we'd feel more comfortable if we could be sure. After all, he did commit perjury before."

"Should I take the test?" I asked Jim Sharp.

"Why not—unless you've got something to hide?"

I didn't, not anymore, so I agreed to the test. Like most people, I had heard of lie detector tests and thought they simply determined whether or not you were telling the truth. While that may be the intention, much additional information is revealed in the process. There is nothing wrong with that, either, except that it's a good idea to have your lawyer present during the testing. I didn't. I didn't think it was necessary, and neither did my lawyers.

An FBI man named Pierce gave me the test, and he was an expert. He was the one who had broken the Yablonski case by testing a woman suspect over a period of two weeks. Later he moved right up the line breaking the other people involved. My test took only two days, but they were among the most uncomfortable days I have ever spent in my life.

Pierce began by asking me a lot of questions that had nothing to do with Watergate. They were personal questions, meant to provoke certain kinds of emotional responses so that eventually they provided a catalog of reactions that were typical of me. Then we went on to Watergate.

It was the first part of the test that was uncomfortable, because I don't like answering personal questions. I don't feel that the answers are anyone's business, and I am sure the graph indicated that I balked. Okay. If I showed the same reaction to a Watergate-related question, they would know I was holding something back. So much for the way the test worked. I understood that, but I still resented being asked about things I preferred to forget. But I reasoned that businessmen have done a few things in their careers that might be considered unethical —although not necessarily illegal—and they don't want to be reminded of them. The same is true of anyone in politics. When everyone is out to win, the game can get pretty rough.

And then we reached the subject of campaign money. Many people knew that a great deal of campaign funds had changed hands during the preparation for the Watergate breakin, but no one was sure how much had been spent and who might still have some of it.

"Did you receive any of this money?" Pierce asked.

"I don't see how that's related to the cover-up," I said.

"Will you answer the question, Jeb?"

"I don't want to."

"Why not?"

"It's irrelevant."

"You're not telling us the truth. Come on, now—how much did you get? "

I leaned back in my chair and groaned. They weren't going to understand the way it happened—and I couldn't exactly blame them.

When I was working for CRP, there was always a great deal of money floating around, not in my department, but in the Finance Committee's area. But if we needed money for anything, we could get it fairly easily.

Just before I left CRP, I confided to Fred LaRue that I thought I might need a lawyer if the Watergate investigation began again. "What if I have to pay some legal fees up front?" I said. "I don't have that kind of money."

When I talked to Mitchell about it, he said, "Don't worry about money. We'll pay your legal fees." Somehow that wasn't good enough. It was too vague. So I went to Haldeman, but he was even more vague. He said he would help me, as a friend, but he couldn't guarantee that the President would, which was Haldeman's way of protecting both the President and himself.

Fred LaRue had given me funds during the campaign for certain expenses, and I had $7,000 left at the time. I paid a few campaign bills with some of it, but I put most of it away, just in case I might need it. I still had it. As far as I was concerned, any

legal fees I might incur would be legitimate campaign expenses.

When I told the story to Pierce, naturally the information was passed on to the prosecutors, and
there were more questions. This time, though, my
lawyers were present.

"You can't keep the money, Jeb," Jim Sharp advised me. "It's okay if CRP wants to pay some of
your legal expenses, but we'll have to work that out
through the normal channels."

Earl Silbert agreed. He seemed to understand
why I had taken the money, but as he explained, it
wasn't going to do me any good, and I might as well
give it back.

I returned the money to CRP immediately and
thought that was the end of the matter. I couldn't
have been more wrong.

As far as the lie detector test was concerned, Silbert, Glanzer, and Campbell were satisfied with the
results. The information confirmed everything I had
told them earlier.

In the spring of '73 Archibald Cox had been appointed Special Prosecutor for the Watergate investigation, but the changes in the staff were not made
immediately. When I began cooperating with the
prosecutors in mid-April, I was still working with
the outgoing team. By May the Cox people replaced
Silbert, Glanzer, and Campbell.

The original prosecutors were fair-minded men.
We would never be friends and they made no bones
about the fact that they wanted to see me in jail, but
there was a certain objectivity in their investigations
that prevented them from taking an accusing
stance. Not so with the Cox team. They were young,
surprisingly inexperienced in the field, and out to
wreak vengeance rather than administer justice.

When I was a member of the White House staff, I was given the impression that no one was just an adversary. There were only "enemies" who were to be destroyed just as mercilessly as if we were meeting them on a battlefield. I was never comfortable with that kind of attitude, which is one of the reasons I got myself off the staff and into the campaign. To me the "enemies" philosophy was something sadly peculiar to the White House, so I was somewhat shocked to find it reappearing in the offices of the prosecutors. Only this time *I* was the enemy.

The fairness, the objectivity and compassion, even the dedication to getting at the truth, were gone. Most of the Cox team had served in the Kennedy and Johnson administrations or were allied with them philosophically, and they approached this one conservative Republican as someone less than human rather than as a man who had broken the law. Their attitude was not, "Tell us the truth about what happened," but "Admit that you haven't told us all the truth." As they went through all the information gathered by Silbert, Glanzer, and Campbell, they gave their own interpretation to the facts.

The results of my lie detector test provided them with a feast. As part of the complete picture of my responses, Pierce had deliberately asked questions designed to draw out any guilty feelings I had about incidents earlier in my career. Now the investigators seized upon those "admissions of guilt" as if they were the complete portrait of Jeb Magruder.

"We know you're not telling us the truth," one of them would say before almost every question, "and we know you can't help it. It's just the way you are —you're a louse." Then came the head-shaking, the tongue-clucking, the arrogant smile so reminiscent of Bob Haldeman. I couldn't believe it—they embodied the very characteristics they so passionately despised.

At first I worked mainly with three people: James Neal, who was second in command to Archibald Cox and the only one of the three who had extensive experience in criminal prosecutions; Richard Ben-Veniste; and Jill Vollner, the only woman on the team. Jim Neal was a former Marine who was more like a caricature of what Marines are supposed to be —and aren't always: an I've-been-around kind of guy, tough and abusive. Rick Ben-Veniste was coarse and nasty. The first time I saw Jill Vollner, she came into the room carrying a pad and pencil and said something about getting a cup of coffee.

"As long as you're going for coffee, would you get some for me? " I requested, thinking she was a secretary.

"I'm not here to run errands for you, Mr. Magruder," she said, and she was good-natured enough to smile. "I'm here as a lawyer." I'm afraid I got off on the wrong foot with her!

It wasn't only the pad and pencil that fooled me. I guess I was guilty of a certain amount of male chauvinism in expecting a woman attorney to look a certain way. Jill wasn't what anyone would call austere. Her skirts were short and she made good use of her femininity among the men on the staff. Although she treated me like a nonperson, by comparison with Neal and Ben-Veniste, she seemed almost pleasant.

I didn't expect special treatment, but I was a cooperating witness who had been placed under my own recognizance. There was no need for them to abuse what little legal power they had over me. Nor was I the only witness they had. John Dean had offered to cooperate a short time before I did, but he was bargaining for immunity. Nevertheless he was giving them enough tidbits to whet their appetite for the banquet he promised. And there were others.

When the prosecutors got some information from a witness, they tried to check it out with the others, so although I had already told the first team everything I knew, I kept being called back to hear what someone else had said. That was when I learned that Larry Higby, Bob Haldeman, and John Dean had taped some of our telephone conversations just before I went to the prosecutors.

Those tapes had been turned over to the investigating team—by whom I don't know—and I think they took some pleasure in playing them for me. It's funny, but even though I had suspected that I was being set up at the time of the conversations, the actual proof of it made me sick. As I listened to the tapes, the trap I had walked into seemed so obvious that I could hardly believe I had not caught on earlier. But what really incensed me was the fact that someone had taped my private conversations. I, who once was in favor of the good guys using wiretaps to get the bad guys, was suddenly furious at this invasion of my privacy—because now that I was about to lose it, privacy was very precious to me.

I began to see the bugging of the Democratic National Committee's office in a totally different light. Suddenly it wasn't "just one of the things you do in a campaign," and I didn't care how many other campaigners had done it before. I was discovering how it *felt,* and it was nothing less than the violation of a human being.

My frequent trips to the prosecutors' offices were eating away at the time I needed to give to my consulting business. Since my clients were widely scattered, I often had to travel, but it was becoming almost impossible to keep my appointments. Neal, Ben-Veniste, and Vollner couldn't have cared less about the fact that my family was going to need financial support during my prison term. If they wanted to see me, they expected me simply to cancel any business appointments I might have made. I tried to explain that I might be able to work things out better if they would give me a little advance notice, and that my concern was not just for myself but for Gail and our children. But I couldn't reach them on that level. Whatever happened to any of us was of no interest to them.

Understandably, they were nervous about the trial, but their anxiety got the better of their judgment. In October of '73, Gail's father offered us some airline tickets to Greece which he was unable to use. He thought Gail would benefit from the change of scene, and I certainly agreed. But the Cox team became almost paranoid about the possibility that once I was out of the country I wouldn't come back, so they refused to allow me to leave. Gail's father tried to assure Archibald Cox's office that the trip was a family vacation, nothing more, and expressed his concern for Gail, but that made no difference. Finally my lawyers appealed to Judge Sirica, who took a more rational view of the matter. He saw that the prosecutors were overstepping their authority and acting as my judges. "Let me be the judge," was Sirica's attitude, and then he granted me permission to make the trip. Summarizing his decision he reminded the prosecutors that I'd had plenty of opportunities to leave the country if that had been my intention, and clearly it wasn't.

Each time I was questioned by the prosecutors, we went through the same old routine. I would answer their questions and then I would be told, "Well, Jeb, you know, you took that seven thousand dollars, and if you could do that, who knows what else you might be hiding?" The context in which the seven thousand dollars was taken, plus the fact that it had been returned to CRP, was ignored.

The manner in which I answered their questions

also bothered them. They preferred working with someone like John Dean, who gave them detail after detail with nothing in between. That just isn't the kind of person I am. I have a marketing background, not a legal one, and I tend to interpret the facts. This made my answers longer and more colored with opinions about how the facts fit together. Over and over I would be interrupted by one of my questioners saying, "Never mind that garbage! Just tell us what happened—who said what and who did what, not *why!*"

I realized that they were concerned about the way I would behave on the witness stand, so I tried to reassure them.

"Don't worry," I kept saying. "I know how I'm supposed to behave in court and I'll be all right." I said it so many times I couldn't stand the sound of the words, but they made no impression. The interruptions continued, and so did the telephone calls insisting that I come to the prosecutors' offices "right now."

They were wearing me down. How could I keep them from consuming the time I needed to make a living while I was still a free man? If I lost the few clients I had, how would I take care of Gail and the children? CRP had made good its earlier commitment to pay my initial legal fees, but there would be more, and how would I pay for them?

Gradually I began to realize that my relationship with the prosecutors was a struggle for survival. In their eyes I was an enemy, and I would be destroyed if I didn't fight back. But how? I spoke to Jim Bierbower and Jim Sharp about my predicament and they decided to complain to the prosecutors. Though I knew that would help, I decided there might be something more immediate that I could do. I could make myself unavailable.

I began avoiding telephone calls from the prosecutors and when I went away on business I left no word where I could be reached. As expected, there was an uproar, but there was very little else anyone could do. The prosecutors had legal authority over me although it would have been difficult for them to exercise it. Also, I wasn't taking a risk with my future, because the length of my prison sentence would be determined by Judge Sirica, not by the investigating team. And from what I was hearing from friends who knew the judge, he wasn't impressed with the abilities of the prosecutors. Their recommendations were not likely to influence his decision, and they would nevertheless have to furnish the standard letter stating that I had cooperated as a witness.

I had one more tactic to use in my defense: if Jill Vollner, Rick Ben-Veniste, and the others were particularly annoying to me, it was obvious that I was capable of infuriating them. So instead of trying to keep my answers down to the bare details, I did just the opposite, I began to elaborate. I wandered from the point, interpreting everything but the punctuation marks, and threw in any opinions that came into my mind. If I was interrupted, I began all over again and made my answer even longer. Finally it was my questioners who began to wither visibly. Later, John Dean was to quote Jim Neal as saying that "Magruder was nothing but a crybaby," and he was absolutely right. I complained, agonized, delayed, and disappeared. I did whatever I could to frustrate them because I no longer believed—as I had at first—that they were there for a good purpose. They were out to destroy me and my family, and I had to fight back.

One day, after two other secondary prosecutors walked out of the room in a huff, I said to Jill Vollner, "Look, the reason we're not getting anywhere is because I can't stand those guys. You seem like a fairly sensitive person. If you can get them off my back, we'll be able to get some work done." That, plus everything else my lawyers and I were doing, seemed to work. Jill Vollner began to put together my testimony alone, while the other prosecutors concentrated on Dean, LaRue, Kalmbach, and the other witnesses.

Though I was surviving, for the first time in my life I couldn't control or prevent any of the things that were happening to me. I could fend off the abuse of the prosecutors, but I couldn't change the fact that my career was ruined, that I was an object of public scorn, that I didn't know how long I would have to be in prison, and that my family's future, as well as my own, was uncertain. I couldn't tell how much damage this experience would do to my children or whether my marriage could withstand the strain.

Whatever was going to happen to me was out of my hands. And that was hard to take, especially for someone who had prided himself on handling his life pretty well up to that point. A few months earlier I would have looked back and taken credit for coming a long way in a very short time. Now I also had to take responsibility for my sudden plunge from near the top of the political ladder.

I thought of the song "My Way" which Frank Sinatra had made popular. I used to call it my theme song—many men do. Well, my way of doing things hadn't been very successful after all. In fact, it had become absolutely disastrous. The ground was caving in under my feet and there was nothing I could grasp to keep myself from falling—into what, I didn't know. I only hoped I wouldn't pull anyone else down with me. But even that was beyond my control.

I felt completely helpless.

3

Louie

ONE SATURDAY EARLY in 1973 I read in the paper that there was a new minister at National Presbyterian Church. He was Dr. Louis H. Evans, Jr., formerly of LaJolla Presbyterian Church in California, and he was going to lead his first service on Sunday. National Pres, as everyone calls the church, wasn't far from our home, so I decided to go and listen to Dr. Evans. He was supposed to be a good preacher.

Dr. Evans was better than good. He was amazing. I couldn't imagine anyone coming to a new congregation and giving a more meaningful message than he did. He said he wanted everyone to know where he was in relation to them. As a man, he said, he

was a human being with shortcomings as well as resources. He couldn't do everything everyone wanted
him to do, nor could he even live up to his own expectations; he couldn't be all things to all people.
But he was a man of God, a husband, a father, and
a minister, and he would do his best to meet his responsibilities in each of those areas. He would give
as much as he could to each of them, but he hoped
he would not allow any one area to consume so
much of him that there would be nothing left to
meet the needs of the others. It was a beautiful way
to say two things—that his personal life would not
come between him and the congregation, and that
he would serve them better if he also had time to
study and be a husband and father.

I liked the way Dr. Evans spoke. He made me feel
as if he were speaking directly to me, and I think
everyone in the sanctuary must have had that same
sense of closeness.

As I left the church that morning I knew that I
wanted to come back soon. Then I became involved
with the prosecutors again and never got to do many
of the things I had planned. It was more convenient
to keep attending services at our own church, where
our children went to Sunday school, than to make a
special effort to visit National Pres. But I didn't forget the impression Dr. Evans had made on me.
There was something about him—something decent
and sincere. I just couldn't quite put my finger on
the special quality that seemed to flow from him to
me.

After the Watergate cover-up broke down, I
found it hard to go to church at all. I was becoming
too well known in a negative way, and being in any
kind of group was uncomfortable. Even in church I
had a feeling that people were looking, pointing,
wondering. I also had the idea that God might be

looking down at me with distaste and thought it better to keep my distance from him.

In June, after I had testified before the Ervin Committee—which was televised—I received a lot of mail, most of it supportive. And there among the letters was one from Dr. Louis Evans and his wife Colleen:

Dear Mr. Magruder,

My husband and I came to Washington only recently. We used to live in LaJolla, California, until Louis was called to serve the congregation of National Presbyterian Church. So we aren't up on all the news here.

But after watching you testify before the Senate Committee on TV today, I felt I had to write to you. Of all the people we have seen or listened to during this tragic time, we seem to feel a special empathy with you. I think we understand something of where you have been and where you are trying to go—because we have seen God use other painful circumstances to offer His love and show us that He can bring goodness out of disaster.

Your family and ours live only a few blocks apart, and since we would really like to get to know you as neighbors, we hope you will stop in whenever you have the time—to talk, to pray, or just to say hello.

God bless you,
Colleen and Louis Evans

It was beautiful, and I said to myself, one of these days I *will* stop in to talk. I hadn't realized until then how much Gail and I needed an opportunity to share what we were feeling with someone who wouldn't push or question or advise, but would simply listen. As the Evanses had sensed, we needed someone who was "just there."

We were able to get away from Washington quite frequently that summer. I had contracted to write a book about Watergate and used part of the advance to rent a house in Blue Ridge Summit, Pennsylvania. Gail and the children spent the whole summer there, and I joined them on weekends. It was a refreshing break from the harassment of the prosecutors.

One Friday afternoon I finished my work earlier than usual and was about to leave town for the weekend when I remembered the letter from the Evanses. I wanted very much to see them, just as I had wanted to go and listen to Dr. Evans' first sermon at National Pres. It was as if someone were trying to tell me something.

I got in my car and drove the few blocks to the Evans' home. Dr. Evans wasn't in, but I met Colleen, and I felt that same undefinable something reaching out from her to me and giving me a feeling of—"all-rightness" is the only way I can describe it. We talked for only a moment at the front door, but I was sure, then, that someone was trying to tell me something. I said I would come back one night the next week and would call before I came.

That was in July. I did return the following week and met Louis—or Louie, as everyone calls him—and we began to talk. We talked about life, about the human experience and the stubbornness of man, about God, his Son, and the Holy Spirit. The wonderful thing was that Louie didn't try to force me into God's arms. He knew such an approach wouldn't have worked with me. I have to reach things intellectually before I can grasp them emotionally. I have to see the logic in everything, even in faith. It wouldn't have done any good for Louie to have explained to me then that God loved me and that I could have a personal relationship with Jesus Christ, because to me it wasn't logical for anyone to love me after what I had done. I wasn't ready for that, and Louie never tried to hurry things.

What he gave me was a kind of friendship I had never known. Instead of "You do this for me and I'll do this for you," his attitude was, "I don't care what you've done, I'm your friend. I love you, brother." He let me know that he would help me in any way he could, but that if I didn't want help, that was okay, too. I didn't have to take—or give—anything. It was enough that *I was*.

Sensing that he had aroused my intellectual curiosity, Louie suggested some books I might like to read. I began with a few by Bruce Larson and went on to the *Barclay Commentaries*. Someone else gave me a copy of Keith Miller's *A Taste of New Wine*. And when Louie referred to scripture passages, he would describe their historical and theological context. That was very important to me. I had read through the Bible periodically and had attended some Bible study courses, but I still found it difficult to pick up the Bible and turn to a passage that had significance for me at a particular moment in my life. When Louie began to explain to me what was going on in the lives of people for whom a certain passage of the Bible had been written, that made a difference. Finally I could relate the deeper meaning of the words to human experiences—eventually to my own.

It was under Louie's leadership that I slowly began to enter a community of Christians I had not known existed. Some of their names were familiar to me, and I had met several of them before, but never on this level. For instance, I had met Doug Coe of Fellowship House when I was on the White House staff and he was organizing weekly prayer breakfasts for people in government. I didn't think one prayer meeting a week was enough to do any lasting good, but it was better than nothing, and the need for spiritual communication was evident. Then I heard that many of the people who attended those breakfasts came away wondering, "Where do we go from here?" When I got to know Doug at Fellowship House and saw his work with small groups, I found the answer to that question. Sharing one's faith with others could lead to an understanding of how that faith makes a difference in a person's life. I was beginning to experience that sharing with Christians like Doug and Louie, Gene Arnold, Bill Brehm, and Donner Buchet.

It was interesting that I was going back over the same ground with both my new friends and the prosecutors, yet their attitudes toward me were entirely· different. To the prosecutors I was dirt, and everything I told them increased their contempt for me. They seemed to make themselves my moral judges and passed sentence on my wrongdoings every day. But my Christian friends made me feel that I was important to them as a person. They didn't condone any of the wrong I had done, but they were concerned about the pain I was experiencing as I faced up to it. I think it was this, more than anything else at the time, that gave me the determination to survive. In the eyes of these friends I was someone created by God and loved by him, and even though I couldn't understand or quite believe how that was possible, I couldn't deny what I felt. Still, no one urged, no one nudged or in any way pushed me to accept the kind of faith they had.

All my life there had been a sort of restlessness inside me. Something wasn't quite right about wherever I was or whatever I was doing. I was never really happy, even though I had everything supposedly necessary to make a person happy. Though I used to think that maybe the next step up the ladder would bring me the missing ingredient, it never did.

And it wasn't missing only in me. I recognized the same symptoms in many of the men I worked with.

I especially remembered the way Richard Nixon had been before he became President. I used to see him at many Republican events, and if ever there was a man driven by a hunger to be President, he was one. So when he was elected in 1968, I thought, *Well, he's got everything he wants now, so he must be happy. Maybe that will happen to me someday.* But it didn't happen to me or to Richard Nixon. He had climbed as high as a man could go, and still he was unsatisfied. He was still driven; he still saw enemies under every bush. I think his occasional outbursts of vindictiveness were expressions of his unhappiness.

So now and then I used to ask myself, "Is there something in life that I'm missing?"

In those days I wouldn't have taken the time to find out. When things were going well, many people think they don't need Jesus Christ, and I might have gone on that way for the rest of my life if it hadn't been for Watergate. I probably would have gone to hear Louie Evans preach, and I'm sure I would have enjoyed knowing him, but that's where it would have stopped. He would have been too "religious" for comfort. No conversations about what Christ really meant in a particular passage of Scripture; no pursuit of an important biblical word to its Greek or Hebrew origins; no exchange of ideas about what Christ is saying to us—or to me as an individual— today. I never would have revealed my spiritual need to anyone in those days. And I think Louie realized that. I think he saw my helplessness as an opportunity for him to minister to me. Thank God he did.

There was no choice left—I had to confront my own inner needs. And I realized I needed a relation-

ship with a higher being. All the earthly supports I
had ever known had given way, and when I saw how
flimsy they were I understood why they had never
been able to make me happy. The missing ingredient in my life was Jesus Christ and a personal relationship with him. Anything else was a great big *if*,
and only he was constant. Whatever I had lost I
could do without. With him I could survive. But the
thing I needed most I had never had, and that was
the knowledge that God loved me, and would never
stop. That awareness could have much to do with
the way I survived.

From the moment I met Louie Evans I began to
experience what unconditional love meant, because
he mirrors it in all his relationships. Other men and
women are his brothers and sisters in Christ: he
loves them unconditionally, yet with a full awareness of their faults and weaknesses. Although his
patience is endless, he can also point out firmly that
while he loves a person, he isn't very happy about
the way that person is behaving.

For a long time I wondered how such a love was
possible, especially when I began to see it in the
friends I met through Louie. Then, very slowly, I
realized that these were not perfect persons and that
they had not been born with this enormous capacity
to love even the most fallen of human beings. What
I was witnessing was the love of God transmitted
through one human being to another. I had heard
the word *instrument* before, but now it was taking
on a form I could recognize. An instrument is simply a human being who knows he is loved by God
and allows that love to influence his relationships
with his fellow men and women. The Evanses and
the Christian community (who had appeared almost
from nowhere to comfort Gail, our children, and
me) were instruments of God's love. Through their

example, I was getting a picture of God himself.

Though I wanted his love to become a part of my life, I thought I wasn't ready for it yet. I had reached the point where I could accept the fact that my Christian brothers and sisters loved me. I couldn't deny it. And they made no bones about the fact that they had their flaws—not as big as mine, as far as I could see, but flaws nevertheless. Jesus Christ was something else. He was a perfect person. He was so flawless that I couldn't find any level on which to communicate with him.

Louie and I used to spend hours discussing what life could be like if it were lived according to the Scriptures. This was no pie-in-the-sky sermonizing. I described to him specific incidents in my past, especially those involving some of the distorted attitudes and misplaced priorities that led up to Watergate—and tried to determine what might have happened if I had made decisions according to Christ's principles instead of my own or someone else's. The difference was amazing—and depressing.

"His way—my way," I said one evening when the contrast was especially painful. "How far apart can you get?"

Louie took a deep breath and closed his eyes for a moment. Then he looked directly at me. "Jeb, you're not *that* far from his way."

I was puzzled. "After what I've done?" I asked.

We were upstairs in Louie's study, a dark-paneled room with a large window and a good view of the winter landscape. To me, the room had a special serenity, but suddenly I couldn't sit still. I began to pace back and forth, from the window to the door, from the door to the window.

"I know I appear pretty calm and collected," I went on. "In fact, many people tell me I seem to be holding up well through all this. But that's only on the surface. Gail and I always have been good at that stiff-upper-lip bit, and that's okay, but I want you to know how things really are." I had never told anyone.

"Louie—I was brought up to be a moral person. And, without waving a flag in anyone's face, I grew up loving this country and what it stands for. I believe in the kind of government we have. And I can't stand knowing that this country has been hurt— that so many people distrust their government and have contempt for some of the people in it—and I had something to do with making it happen. Now that's a long way from the kind of life Jesus Christ would have wanted me to lead—and it's going to take me a long time to close the distance between us."

"How are you going to do that, Jeb?" Louie asked softly. "What do you think you can do to close that distance?"

I shook my head. "I'm not sure, but I have to do something—something worthwhile."

"Aren't you going to let Christ do anything?" he probed.

"Eventually," I said, and we let it go at that.

Louie and I had begun talking in September. Now it was February. The calls from the prosecutors were becoming less frequent, and one day soon I would have to go to prison. Not knowing exactly when that would be made it difficult—for me and for my family. Whenever we tried to look ahead, there was always that prison sentence in front of us. I wasn't eager to go in, but I did want to get it behind me. So I asked my lawyers to present my request for sentencing to the prosecutors and Judge Sirica. At least that would give my future a distinguishable horizon.

By that time the meetings with our Christian

friends had become the most important times of our lives. Colleen had sensed Gail's inner distress and was giving to her the warm and loving support Louie was giving to me. The Evans's youngest son, Jim, was the same age as Whitney, our oldest, and went to the same school. Each relationship seemed to lead to others. Colleen asked Gail to join a covenant group with several other women, many of them wives of the men I had met through Louie. Jim Evans and Whit had become close friends and this friendship was important to Whit during my time in prison.

Quietly, without any fanfare, God seemed to be providing us with the strengths of others at a time when our own strengths were completely drained. In fact, as much as I dreaded going to prison, I felt as if I was being prepared for it, at least as far as my anxiety about my family was concerned.

We felt no sense of indebtedness; it wasn't like receiving money you knew you would have to repay some day. Nor were our friends any poorer for the love and comfort they gave us. They never made us feel as if they were going out of their way to be there when we needed them. Sometimes they surprised us by finding things in us that matched their own needs. I'll always remember the time Louie Evans said to me, "You know, Jeb, I'm new to this political environment. I feel as if there's a lot of ministering that needs to be done in this town, but it's hard to know exactly where to begin. Maybe you can help me see where the big problems are."

With that simple request Louie let me know that I had something of value to give him—that Watergate had not wiped out all of my years of political experience. Something good was left. The fact that he could see it in me revived something I thought was long dead—a small measure of self-respect.

I felt the same kind of acceptance from Gene, Bill, Donner, and the other Christian men with whom I was meeting regularly. I never had the feeling that I was "passing my hat" among them for donations, but rather that we were freely exchanging our thoughts and experiences. There was an openness about our conversations that was different from any other relationships I had known. We could say anything and know we would not be criticized or judged.

Perhaps what was most important, at least for me, was the spirit of confidentiality among us. Each of us knew that whatever any of us said would go no further than that room, and for me this was a special blessing. Gail and I were feeling haunted by the press to the point where we were reluctant to talk to anyone. Some of the stories about us were true, but many were inaccurate, distorted, and even false. We were news, and the reporters had to get the story, but sometimes in their eagerness they went too far. One reporter began calling the neighborhood children, asking, "How are the Magruder kids getting along these days?" Another time a client's employee asked me how I was feeling, and I said I was a bit apprehensive about the Watergate case. A few days later my remark appeared in a newspaper. So the experience of being able to describe how we felt, without fearing that the words would be repeated, helped to ease our tension.

Before I became involved, one group of men had been meeting about once a week at Fellowship House. As the group increased in number, and as more men expressed interest in participating, Louie thought the time was right to form more covenant groups similar to those he had worked with in La-Jolla. The men were already observing several of the basic principles of these groups: being available to each other in time of need, accepting each other exactly as they were, trying to sense each other's inner needs, speaking freely and openly—or not at all, if they chose—and keeping their discussions confidential. But there were too many who wanted to be involved for it to function as effectively as it did at first. So it was decided to form several groups from the original one. Louie made sure he was the leader of the group of which I became a part.

It was on a cold night in March when we made this decision to form several covenant groups. We had met at Fellowship House. Louie had picked me up in his tiny Toyota—whose fuel economy he enjoyed and whose motor he personally kept in perfect tune—and we were quite late getting back. Everyone had been excited about the covenant groups and there was much to talk about. Our enthusiasm made the drive home seem so short that we sat in the car talking after we got to my house. The night air was growing colder as we sat there, under the glow of the streetlight, but it felt good. Louie is six feet two and I'm the same, and with both of us pretzeled into the Toyota, there wasn't much space left.

"I've been wanting to get these groups started ever since I came here, Jeb," Louie exulted. "Wait till you see what the Holy Spirit can do in them!" Then he noticed that I wasn't talking any more. "Something's bothering you," he said.

"You still think I should be in the group?"

"I do."

"But you know I don't feel the same way you do. I might hold the others back."

"We've all been over the same road you're on, Jeb. Some of us found more potholes—some less. But the road was the same. You're not going to hold anyone back."

It was too dark for Louie to see the expression on my face, but he is especially sensitive.

"You still think God won't accept you, don't you?" he asked. I nodded.

"You know, Jeb, your problem is that you still think you have to do twenty years' penance before you can even ask his forgiveness. Well, that just isn't true. He already has forgiven you—and Jesus Christ can tell you that, if you'll allow him to."

"It's that easy?" I questioned. I wanted it so badly, but there was still that risk of being rejected.

"It's *this* easy, Jeb—all you have to do is ask Christ, right now, to forgive you. Tell him that you accept him and ask him if he accepts you." He bowed his head. "I think we ought to pray about it."

I bowed my head. As Louie prayed that Christ would remove my fear and doubt, I found myself speaking to Christ as if he were in the car with us. Never before had I spoken to him so directly: but I'd never felt as if Christ were that close to me, either. I didn't think before I spoke. I simply let the words come out.

I don't remember exactly what those words were, but I know I asked God to forgive me. I said I wanted to give my life to Christ and asked him if he would accept me.

Both of us were silent. Then Louie asked, "Jeb, what did he say?"

"He said yes! Just like that—as clearly as anything I ever heard. He said it was okay!"

"See! What did I tell you!" Louie said.

I leaned back as far as the Toyota would allow. A feeling of relaxation was beginning to replace my excitement. I couldn't remember ever feeling so good. It was similar to the way I had felt when I realized that my Christian brothers and sisters loved me—only much more overwhelming.

"There's more to it, Jeb," Louie went on. "You don't just walk off into the sunset now that you know God loves you."

"Okay, tell me," I urged.

"You've just given your life to Jesus Christ," he pointed out, "and that means there are certain things he wants you to do."

"But I *want* to do them, Louie!"

"Not so fast," Louie cautioned, holding up his hand. He knew I had a hard time being patient. We had talked about it enough times. "First you have to understand *what* he wants you to do. None of us is able to do all he expects us to do, but at least we'd better be trying, because that's part of being a Christian. It isn't enough for us to go to Bible study classes and have fellowship with each other. Those things are good, and I hope you'll keep doing them. But now you have to start doing everything Christ's way—your whole life may have to change as you begin to understand what he wants you to do."

"How can I find that out?" I asked.

"The same way you just found out that he loves you and forgives you—you ask him. But give him time to answer. Sometimes he doesn't tell you right away. And don't expect your life to change overnight."

"Okay," I answered. "It looks as if I'll have to start learning how to be patient."

I thought about Louie's words as I walked from the car to my house. Probably I'll remember them for the rest of my life.

Gail opened the door and I could see she was concerned. She had seen the car parked at the curb all that time. I stood in the hallway, enjoying the warmth and comfort of the house, and started to take off my coat. Then I couldn't wait any longer. I told her what had happened to me.

Gail has a lovely smile that begins slowly—and it was beginning now. "Well," she said, "it's about time."

4

Daddy, Why Do You Have to Go to Prison?

LOUIE WAS RIGHT. My life didn't change overnight. But I knew immediately that there *was* a difference. At first it was more evident to me than to anyone else. Outwardly, everything was still the same—I got up the next morning, ate my breakfast, and went to work. But I didn't look in the mirror and find my features altered. There were no momentous pronouncements to make. I simply began to pay more attention to what I was doing, and why. The first thing I noticed was a sort of objectivity about myself, almost as if I was able to stand back and watch what was going on in my life. Some things weren't important any longer and others began to take their place.

My work has always been important to me, but until Christ entered my life I had never realized how much of my time I was putting into my job. I've always liked my work, and that was fine. But suddenly I didn't think it was right to put it before my family, which I had done many times. Gail and the children needed more of my time than I was giving them, and I needed theirs, so that meant I had to rearrange my priorities.

Without Christ, I wouldn't have been as sensitive to those needs before. And I certainly wouldn't have done anything about them if someone had pointed them out to me. Getting ahead took just about everything out of me, and I didn't want to admit that I came home empty. Now I was beginning to feel more of what others were feeling, especially those close to me. To some people that may seem a small discovery, but to me it was amazing. It was one of the ways Christ was beginning to make his demands on me. He was telling me that being a husband and father had to come before my career.

"Becoming a Christian does make you feel more deeply," Louie said when I told him what was happening. "But it isn't all joyful, Jeb. You'll become more sensitive to pain, and injustice, and frustration. That's Christ in us, too—opening us up to all the human vibrations."

The anxiety of the post–Watergate days had brought Gail, the children, and me closer together, and we needed each other's strength. With the shadow of a prison sentence hanging over us, it was especially important for me to give them as much time as I could. I would be able to do my work well enough without putting in such long hours.

We had never tried to hide from our children the fact that "Daddy would have to go to prison one of these days," and occasionally we reminded them of it so it wouldn't come as a shock to them. Whitney and Justin, who were then thirteen and eleven, understood what that meant, and I think Tracy did, too, although she was only ten at the time. But Stuart, our youngest, was only six and a half, and it was impossible to prepare him for the impending separation. Consequently, he was the one about whom I worried the most.

Naturally there were questions. Whit and Justin wondered why only some of us were going to prison. "Why isn't Haldeman going? Or Ehrlichman, or Mitchell? What about the President?" They were also reading newspaper accounts of questionable practices that had gone on in other administrations, and they asked why nothing was being done about them.

I tried to answer all their questions as honestly as I could. "Some people don't get punished for doing something wrong," I explained, "and there isn't anything we can do about that. But I think it's right that I should go to prison for what I did, because our system of justice would be hurt if I didn't."

"But the system isn't always right," Whit argued.

"I know, and I don't always agree with it, but I do believe in it. And I think that if you compared it to others in this world, you'd probably find it was the best one around."

The hardest question to answer was: "Dad, how long will you have to be in prison?" We hadn't heard from Judge Sirica about the date for sentencing, and we could only guess at the length of the sentence. Bud Krogh had been given six months, and my lawyers and I thought that might be a pretty good guideline.

At no time did we delude ourselves into thinking I might get off with something like probation, although that would not have been an unusual sentence for a charge of obstructing justice. But there were too many political overtones to everything connected with Watergate. The public outcry would have been too alarming—and perhaps justly so. Resentment against the President was beginning to mount, and since he was beyond reach, the full force of public anger fell on us.

That resentment intensified in March of 1974 when the first transcripts of the White House tapes were made public. As curious about what they said as anyone else, I spent a whole weekend sitting on the living room couch, going through them.

The tapes of 21 June 1973, only two days after the Watergate breakin, confirmed my belief that the President knew about the cover-up, and, in fact, had helped to construct it. Actually I was not shocked by the President's language. I had been in his presence at times when he used four-letter words and expressions that he avoided in public, but those times were infrequent. In fairness to him, I felt that the White House tapes revealed him during a time of extreme stress and I don't consider the language typical.

What really hit me hard was the way the President felt about some of the people who had served him and loved him. One of the most extraordinary things about Richard Nixon was his ability to arouse intense feelings of loyalty and devotion in the men and women around him. While he was not a demonstrative man, nor even a particularly friendly person, there were many of us who would have done almost anything to help him or please him.

It wasn't that we never questioned what we were asked to do, but the answer always seemed to be that whatever we were asked to do was right because this man was so right. Our overriding ambition—and I think it surpassed any of our personal ambitions—was to love this man almost as a son wants to love his father.

Bob Haldeman especially reflected this desire, and those of us who worked with Haldeman caught it from him. But there were others, too. John Mitchell was one. Certainly Nixon wasn't a father-figure to him: if anything, it was the other way around. Before Nixon became President, Mitchell was his sponsor and a senior member of the law firm where Nixon was a partner. But while Mitchell's devotion was more fatherly than filial, it was unwavering. Mitchell was more than the Attorney General and director of the campaign. The peacemaker among the rival factions in the Nixon administrations, he was the one who negotiated the bitter differences between Henry Kissinger and Secretary of State William Rogers. Kissinger was impatient with Rogers and had open contempt for his abilities. Rogers resented being kept out of so many foreign policy decisions—only Mitchell was able to calm him down.

As I read the transcripts of what had been going on in the White House a year earlier, when I was deciding to go to the prosecutors, I couldn't help but cry. At first the President referred to me as a "real stand-up guy," one of the true heroes of the administration—which, translated, meant that I was continuing to lie and cover up. Then, as soon as it became obvious that I wouldn't lie anymore, it was: "Magruder's getting weak"; "Yeah, he's that kind of guy—not too bright . . . it looks like we've got problems with Magruder." After I went to the prosecutors I was described with venom and profanity as the President and his closest associates made plans to protect themselves from me. "That phone call I taped will beat the socks off Magruder," John Ehrlichman gloated.

There was no understanding of the situation Fred LaRue and I were in. There was no realization that we *had* to cooperate with the prosecutors, although we had tried to make that clear to people like Haldeman and Mitchell. I remembered the way Fred and I had talked about protecting the others as much as we could, because they were people we cared for and wanted to help. We thought they knew we were in a box, but instead they were attempting to place the blame first on me, then on John Dean, and, if necessary, on "the big enchilada"—John Mitchell.

It was painful to read those transcripts and know the words were spoken by a man you loved. The terminology was ugly, and no one was spared. Some of the President's closest, most loyal supporters were described by him as "second-rate," "jerks," and worse. What deeply disturbed me was not so much the coarseness of the language, although that was bad, but the fact that the President was using those words against his friends.

As it turned out, though, he didn't have many friends. Not really.

Early in May 1974, Judge Sirica informed my lawyers that he would sentence me on May 21. Sharp and Bierbower were pretty sure I would be sent to Allenwood, a minimum security prison in Pennsylvania, which was the usual destination for people sentenced to three years or less. And three years was about the maximum I expected to get. That, I thought, would make me eligible for parole in a year.

Jim Sharp put me in touch with a few men who had been in Allenwood so that I would know what to expect when I arrived there. It helped, but there is no way you can understand what prison is really like ahead of time. It just doesn't seem real until it happens. Nevertheless, I appreciated Jim's concern and I did get some advice that turned out to be helpful later.

One day Jim called me up and said, "Jeb, remember I told you I've been handling Clifford Irving's case?"

"Yes," I said. We had talked about the peculiarities of the case, which involved both Irving and his wife, and the strange autobiography of Howard Hughes.

"He just got out of prison and he's in town," Jim said. "He was at Allenwood for a while, and it might be good for you to talk to him. He's a little different from the others you've talked to, because he got a lot of publicity—like you. Can you be at my office this afternoon?"

"Sure," I promised.

Clifford Irving was already in Jim's office when I got there. Irving was tall, slim, and good-looking, with light brown hair, dark, intelligent eyes, and a casual manner. He dressed well and I guessed he was in his early forties. Though he was friendly and easy to talk to, he wasn't about to let me know how he really felt about things. Almost everything he said came out humorously, which was all right, because his emotions were his own business. I appreciated his willingness to help.

"It's not all that bad, you know," he told me with a slight smile. "The accommodations are fairly clean, the beds aren't lumpy, the food is—edible. No room service, of course." He waved his hand in the air. "There's only one real problem," he said, and when he had my full attention he went on— "boredom!"

"I expect that," I said.

"But you can't possibly expect *how* boring," he

went on. "For six months I was in absolute limbo. About the only thing prison did for me was to bore me—almost to death." He glanced at Jim and then again at me. "I don't know what I'm supposed to learn from that, do you?" His laughter put all of us at ease.

There were other things he had to say, things I would remember later when they really counted. He was a trained observer and had reached conclusions that few prison inmates might have been able to offer me.

"Watch out for cliques," he warned me. "Prison's full of them and it's the fastest way to get into trouble. The blacks, the whites, the Spanish-speaking prisoners—they all form their own groups, and no two of them get along. The best thing you can do is mind your own business and don't get too close to anyone.

"Your notoriety will be a problem, at first. Some of those men have been away from the outside world so long that they'll forget you're not on the White House staff any more. They'll come to you and ask you for favors; they'll want you to use your influence to get them out."

For all his casualness, Clifford Irving was having a hard time picking up his life again. His personal situation was especially difficult because his wife also was in prison. Their children were staying with friends. I wished him luck.

"The boredom—that's your enemy," he repeated as we shook hands and said good-by.

I'd never had much spare time on my hands, and I wondered how it would feel to have nothing to do for days or months. In one sense, I thought, it might be good—it would give me a chance to think and study. Louie and I were working on a list of books for me to read, and I was accumulating a large library to take with me. I might never again have such an opportunity to get into some deep theological reading. Prison wasn't going to be pleasant, but at least I could put the time to good use.

On Tuesday, 21 May 1974, the sentence was pronounced. The proceeding, which we had half-dreaded, half-wanted to happen, for almost a year and a half, was over in about ten minutes.

Louie and Colleen Evans went with us to my lawyers' office where Jim Bierbower and Jim Sharp met us. Then we went to the Court House. Other friends also joined us. Reporters and photographers jammed the doorway, but the photographers were not permitted inside the building. Judge John J. Sirica entered the room and the court was in session.

Even though the judge was reputed to be tough—"Hangin' John" they called him—he was not without compassion. We had heard that he was having a difficult time deciding about sentences for those involved in Watergate. He was concerned about the families of men sentenced to prison and realized that in a very real sense they shared the penalty.

Jim Sharp made his final plea. "I respectfully suggest," he said, "that Mr. Magruder has been serving a sentence for the past thirteen months. He has exposed himself and his family to a year of unremitting humiliation and contempt. And he watched, helpless to protect them, as his wife and children were forced to share his disgrace.

"We ask one thing of the court, considering that Mr. Magruder must be punished, but at the same time realizing that he has remorse and contrition. We ask your honor that when you sentence him here today, that you not knock him down to the point that he cannot get up again, that you leave him with an opportunity to survive this."

Judge Sirica looked at me. "Does the defendant have anything to say before I pronounce sentence?" he asked.

The question was a formality rather than a last-minute chance for the defendant to persuade the judge to go easy on his sentence. (Later, among all my prison acquaintances, I came across only one man whose statement did, in fact, lead to a shorter sentence.) But I did have something to say. I had written it out and brought it with me:

"Your honor, it has been nearly impossible for me to face the disappointment I see in the eyes of my friends, the confusion I see in the eyes of my children, the heartbreak I see in the eyes of my wife, and, probably more difficult, the contempt I see in the eyes of others."

Gail was sitting two rows behind me and I could feel her eyes on me. I was speaking as much to her as to the court.

"I was ambitious, but I was not without morals or ethics or ideals," I said. "There was in me the same blend of ambition and altruism that I saw in many of my peers.

"Somewhere between my ambition and my ideals I lost my ethical compass. I found myself on a path that had not been intended for me by my parents or my principles—or by my own ethical instincts. It has led me to this courtroom.

"I have spent time trying to find out where I lost my way and why. I think I now know. My ambition obscured my judgment.

"I know what I have done, and your honor knows what I have done. I cannot measure the impact on this administration or on this nation of Watergate. But whatever the impact, I am confident that this country will survive its Watergates and its Jeb Magruders."

Like the first part of the proceeding, the rest was quite methodical. Judge Sirica waited barely a second before he said "Jeb Stuart Magruder, I sentence you to from ten months to four years in prison. . . ."

There was more, but I was unable to comprehend it until later. My attention focused on the words "ten months"—*that's good!* I thought. Then I heard "to four years"—*no, it's bad, very bad,* I realized. He could have given me five years, but I was hoping for three or less, so it was a stiff sentence after all.

My mind had detoured and I was unable to catch up with the rest of the sentence. The judge had recommended that I serve my time at Allenwood, which was a break. Usually a man sentenced to more than three years is committed to a "heavy," or maximum security institution, which would have been much worse. Allenwood was not only minimum security, but it was within driving distance of our home so that Gail would be able to visit me. My sentence was to begin June 4, two weeks away.

Before we left the courtroom Gail and I spent a few minutes in an anteroom. Later we were described by the press as "impassive," "unmoved," "in control," but in the privacy of that small room we both broke down. It was just as well, because there was a crowd of reporters and photographers waiting for us at the door of the Court House. It was better to get the tears out of our systems before facing them. Within five minutes we were "impassive," "unmoved," and "in control" again. I said a few innocuous words to reporters on the way out—something to the effect that I had expected to go to prison—but I don't remember them. As I read the report in the newspaper later that day and the next morning, it was as if someone else had spoken them.

The difference between ten and forty-eight months was enormous, not only in terms of my financial provision for Gail and the children, but in the way we would prepare for the separation. Should we set our minds on being apart for ten months or for forty-eight? It was impossible to prepare for something so indefinite.

For some reason we still did routine things that day. It was as if each of us might come apart if we didn't cling to what was normal. My aunt and uncle, the Woolvertons, who also lived in Washington, took us out to lunch at Normandy Farms in the Potomac area north of the District. Gradually our conversation began to include references to prison, even a few awkward attempts to joke about it. (Jim Sharp had explained to us that Judge Sirica had recommended I be considered for parole after serving ten months, which was encouraging. But there was also that growing possibility of serving four years. Of course, as my lawyers were quick to explain, that was a maximum sentence. Even if a parole didn't come through, I could, with good behavior, be out in thirty-two months at the longest. That was still a blow.)

After lunch we went home and told the children what had happened. By then we had absorbed some of our disappointment and, hopefully, didn't pass it on to them. They seemed to accept the sentence, that is, all except Stuart, to whom the whole matter was a distressing intrusion by an adult world that made no sense to him. "Daddy," he said to me, "*why* do you have to go to prison? I make mistakes all the time, and I don't have to go to prison."

Bad as I felt, I had to smile at that. "This is a different kind of mistake, Stuart," I tried to explain, looking for a way to bridge the gap between his logic and mine. I didn't want to brush off his concern with something like: "You'll understand when you get a little older," which wouldn't necessarily be true.

"Your daddy made a mistake that was illegal—that's why it's different. And when a person makes an illegal mistake, he has to go to prison. But after that, he can come back home again."

While Stuart still wasn't satisfied with the explanation, he was working on it—I could see that. If he hit any more snags, he would speak up; he and Whitney were more likely to put their feelings into words, whereas Tracy and Justin kept their emotions to themselves. Gail was quiet, too, but I knew that beneath that calm exterior there was great sensitivity and pain.

That evening as we talked and laid out tentative plans for the months ahead, I felt as if something in me was opening up and reaching out to draw my family very close to me. I seemed to be a part of each one of them, and all of them at the same time, loving them more than ever before and sharing their hurt. It was a deepening of that ability to experience what was going on in another person—"the human vibration," as Louie called it. But even more than that, I was able to give something of myself that had never even been in me before. Ironically, at that particular time I had nothing of my own left to give to those I loved. Then I realized what was happening. It was Christ in me I was able to give; in fact, it was he who was doing the giving—through me.

It was growing dark and Gail moved about the room, closing the curtains and turning on the lamps. The light brought warmth into the room. I looked at my wife and wondered if I had ever really known her before. We had been married almost fifteen years, and in that length of time a couple ought to know just about everything there is to know about each other, right down to moods, quirks, and how-do-you-like-your-eggs? But the crises in our lives had been few until then, and there was much about each of us still undiscovered. How fortunate I was that everything I was discovering about Gail was good, strong, and beautiful.

Through all the strain of the post-Watergate months she was more than my wife. She was my friend. There rarely were any accusations or regrets; she would not play the martyr. As frightened and concerned as she was about our future, she was always able to come up with words of encouragement and comfort, and sometimes—I don't know how—with humor. Her judgment about some of the events and attitudes leading up to Watergate had been sounder than mine, but she was kind enough never to wave that in front of my nose. And I don't think she refrained out of a sense of righteousness. She simply wasn't preoccupied with the past. Her thoughts ran to the future and the big question about the kind of life we might have—someday.

As I thought about the two of us I saw that it wasn't so unusual for us to feel both familiar and unknown to each other. Gail had accepted Christ just before I did, so in that sense both of us were new creations. Like me, she looked about the same and did many of the same things at the same times, but inside something new was being born. It would take time for each of us to become acquainted with that newness in the other and to build our lives around it. In addition, there was a great deal of debris from the past in our relationship. It had to be cleared out piece by piece. So after almost fifteen years we were, in a sense, starting our marriage over again.

I knew that everything happening to us wasn't happening *just* to us. The people who loved us, our friends, our covenant brothers and sisters, even some perfect strangers, were truly sharing what we were going through and giving us their own strength when ours ran out. Their phone calls, their letters and words of comfort—the fact that they were there —made all the difference.

Not all of our political friends turned away. Some stood by us throughout the Watergate experience— Lydia and Rob Odle, Dolores and Bob Morgan, Joan and Bob Marik, Bob Frank, John Evans, and Harry Dent. During the past five years I have worked with some of them on several consulting projects.

There were many personal friends of the family who gave us their love and support in those days— Blaney and Nini Colmore (he was an Episcopal minister who was very close to me); Harry and Didi Rieger, good friends from Philadelphia; Don Atha, an old friend who assisted me financially while I was in prison; Carl Vogt, a fraternity brother who is now a Washington lawyer working with Leon Jaworski. Many of these friends also visited me in prison. Guilda and David Herndon were early Washington friends who stayed close to us. David, a lawyer, helped advise me on my legal problems. Mike and Jane Deland were from Boston. While playing football at Harvard Mike had been injured so that now he has to use crutches to walk. His attitude and strength in adversity were awesome. Mike was an inspiration to me.

These friends taught me an important lesson in love and friendship. It seems to me that sometimes, in our spiritual fervor, we Christians are tempted to believe that our only support during the hard times comes from other committed Christians. This is not always so. Not all those who stood by me were Christians—but all of them accepted me as their brother, and I don't ever want to forget that.

A few days after I was sentenced, Don Riegle, *Democratic* Congressman from Michigan, a man I had never met, sent me a note:

> . . . I have followed your situation for some months . . . and my thoughts are with you and your family.
>
> We all make mistakes—and I hope when this period is over, you and your family can look forward to better and happier days.
>
> As difficult as the immediate future may seem, it will pass—and there is a long road ahead.
>
> Despite whatever our past differences may have been. . . . If I can be of help at some point, let me know.

I was surprised by a letter from Chuck Colson, written the day after I was sentenced:

> Dear Jeb—
>
> I have delayed writing to you until now on the grounds that any communication might be misunderstood by the prosecutors. I just want you and Gail to know that you were both very much in our hearts and prayers yesterday. I know that you can handle what lies ahead and in some ways you are perhaps better off than the rest of us, since at least there is now some certainty about your future. You can begin to plan a new life; we sincerely hope, Jeb, that it will be a full and rewarding life for you and Gail.
>
> You and I have had our differences in the past and while I haven't read your book, I understand it contains some less than flattering references to me. Maybe they are deserved, maybe not—that is really irrelevant. We have both been through that and I suspect we both have very different views of ourselves, our families and the world we live in. I have learned to live without personal animosities, and for whatever feelings I've had in the past, I hope you will forgive me.

What really prompts me to write is that mutual friends have told me that you have accepted Christ in your life and that Gail has as well. Let me tell you that, if so, you are born again and you will be free, no matter what.

Patty said she sees Gail at her Bible class from time to time. If we can help Gail at any time, tell her please to let Patty know. God will be with you, Jeb, no matter what happens. Good luck and don't despair.

I had heard about Chuck's commitment to Christ from Doug Coe and Harold Hughes, and I had mixed feelings about him. I was happy for Chuck because I knew that he would become a powerful Christian witness. There would be wonderful ways for him to use his exceptional abilities. But again there was that matter of debris from the past: Chuck and I interpreted events differently, and the confrontation had left its wounds on both of us. Perhaps the only kind of relationship we could have for some time would be through our love for Christ, which actually isn't a bad place to begin. I appreciated Chuck's letter and knew that his offer to help was genuine.

Another surprise was a note from Barbara Walters who had interviewed Gail a few days before I was sentenced:

At last your wait is over. Knowing you and your family, I felt relief that the sentence was no longer, and pain that it was as long as it is.

I know your love and courage will see you through the long months and that finally, when the months are over, you will indeed, deservedly, live happily ever after.

So, although I did have to go to prison, I was taking with me more love and friendship than I had

ever known. Spiritually speaking, I was anything
but alone.

Gail and I were able to get away by ourselves for
a few days, and then I spent the rest of the time putting my affairs in order so that she would be able to
take over the financial management of the family. I
gave Gail my power of attorney and explained how
she should handle any matters related to my consulting business which, of course, I was giving up. I
went over our bank accounts with her and made out
a schedule of dates when certain bills had to be
paid. Budgeting would be important because we
didn't know how far we would have to stretch the
money we had saved. And there was always the unexpected expense.

During the last few days before turning myself in
at Allenwood prison I read and reread a newspaper
column written by Kenneth Eskey, a Scripps-How-
ard staff writer who was one of my covenant brothers. It was important to me, not only because of the
insight Ken had into my situation, but because he
was able to express so simply and accurately the
special covenant relationship:

> They sentenced Jeb Stuart Magruder to 10 months
> in prison the other day for his role in the Watergate
> cover-up.
> It was no surprise, really. He knew it was coming.
> But it means we won't be seeing Jeb on Thursday
> mornings for a while. That's too bad. He was a loyal
> member of the 7:30 A.M. coffee-and-doughnut bri-
> gade.
> Which is to say that 10 of us have been meeting for
> breakfast every Thursday morning in Louie's study.
> Nothing fancy. Just an hour or so of sticky rolls and
> quiet conversation.
> Louie, as it happens, is pastor of the National Pres-

byterian Church. He's a strong, sensitive man who
gives a great deal of himself. Like all of us, he needs a
great deal of love and affection in return.

Mostly we talk at breakfast about each other's problems, which don't amount to much when you consider the problems of humanity in general.

Lately it's Jeb we've been concerned about. Not because we admire the things he did. He was wrong and
he knows it. But because he's a husband, and a father
of four children, who's about to spend the better part
of a year in jail.

It's a strange sensation to break bread with a man
one day, and know he'll be gone the next.

The rest of us, no doubt, will conduct Thursday
morning business as usual while Jeb's at Allenwood,
serving his sentence.

We're an odd group in some ways: two home build-
ers, a computer salesman, an assistant secretary of
defense, a newpaperman, a preacher, an overworked
patent lawyer, a young banker whose wife may be expecting twins, an ex-bureaucrat who's trying to raise
money for a struggling missionary corps.

What we share is a commitment to care about each
other. It sounds corny, Joe Kool, but it's true.

Oh, yes, we have the normal aggravations—
depressed wives, uptight children, high blood pressures, not enough money, not enough time, anxieties,
frustrations.

But things always seem a little less bleak, somehow,
after one of those Thursday morning breakfasts in
Louie's study.

Drop in when you get back, Jeb.

5

Allenwood

ALLENWOOD FEDERAL PRISON CAMP is five miles north of Lewisburg Penitentiary in north central Pennsylvania and is part of the same prison system. Lewisburg is the heavy institution, its gray buildings surrounded by a thirty-foot-high concrete wall and watchtowers. The guards are armed. Every window is barred. The inmates, most of them sentenced to long terms for violent crimes, spend their days and nights in six-by-nine-foot cells which are locked up for the night at 11 P.M. There isn't much for a man to do.

At Allenwood there is no outer wall and the guards are not armed. Part of its 4200 acres of Pennsylvania farmland is enclosed by a six-foot-high wire fence, which you don't even notice once you're inside the place. The immediate area around the administration building and the dormitories on a hill behind it has been cleared of trees and bushes, which leaves it looking a bit naked. That bareness is about the only sign of a security precaution.

The inmates sleep in eight dormitories—two dorms to a building, fifty-four men to a dorm—and except at certain count-times they can move about freely from one building to another. There are jobs of a sort for everyone. The warden speaks with pride about two tennis courts (one indoors also used as a basketball court), a baseball field, a library, and, about a mile down the dirt road to the right, a church. In each building there is a room where men can watch TV, play Ping-Pong and cards. Once a week there is a movie.

The countryside around Allenwood is absolutely beautiful, especially in the summertime, which is when I first saw it. Everywhere you look there are rounded green hills, many of them thick with trees. Bordering part of the prison camp property is a public golf course which some passersby take to be part of the prison itself. No one is surprised by this impression because Allenwood has the reputation of being a very unusual penal institution. It has been labeled a "country club prison" by those who have taken a tour through its facilities, pronouncing them relatively luxurious, considering that they are intended for criminals. "White-collar prison" is another of Allenwood's labels, again the contribution of various prison-browsers who mistakenly concluded that most of the inmates come from white-collar backgrounds rather than traditional criminal habitats.

There are eleven minimum-security prisons in the United States, housing about 3400 inmates. Allenwood's population is usually about 375 men.

The reason why there are no concrete walls or watchtowers manned with guns is that there is practically no need for such things in this kind of prison. The inmates are serving short sentences, usually for nonviolent crimes, and they have no desire to add to their time in prison by attempting to escape. They also know that such rash behavior will get them sent up the road to Lewisburg. Now and then someone "walks away" (the term used for a prisoner who leaves with the intention of returning), usually because there are problems at home and no one to help solve them. But almost every time the "walkaway" comes back of his own free will, in which case the intention to return is taken into consideration. Sometimes only a little extra time is added to the sentence, but the inmate is always transferred to another institution, often to a "heavy" one.

On our way to Allenwood on June 4, Gail and I passed Lewisburg penitentiary. Even from a distance it was grim, and I could understand why a man wouldn't want to end up there.

"That's yours," Benny said, pointing to the bunk. We both had been silent as we walked up the hill from the administration building to the assignment and orientation dormitory. A guard had turned me over to Benny, and at first I didn't know whether he was a guard or a prisoner. Later I would learn to distinguish between them by the way they dressed: the guards wore gray denim uniforms and the inmates wore surplus army khakis. In many other ways it was hard to tell them apart because the guards were also victims of the prison atmosphere and developed some of the same characteristics as the inmates.

I had just gone through "Administration and Documentation." I'd been fingerprinted and given a number—00582-134. After I had stripped and been given a body search, I dressed in khakis that were too small for me. Gail and I had said a troubled good-by and she had taken my civilian clothes home. When she left, I felt as if my identity went out the door with her.

I nodded to Benny as he left. It was a few minutes before 4 P.M. The dorm was half-empty and there seemed to be many men on their way in. Carrying sheets and a blanket and a pillow for the bed, I also had a box of books and some underwear which the guards had said I could bring in with me. (I was lucky; sometimes they said no, I had been told.) I started to make up my bed, just to have something to do. Then I put my box under the bed.

"You don't want to do that," someone said. It was the man in the bunk across from mine. He was in his late forties and wore glasses. When I looked up at him he came over.

"Use one of the cabinets if you want to hold onto those things," he said, pointing to the metal cabinets at each end of my bed. "Put that box under your bed and somebody'll steal it right out from under you while you sleep."

"Thanks," I replied, and pulled the box toward me.

"Ask one of the guards for a lock for your cabinets," he went on. "Keep your clothes there, and anything else you don't want to lose." He held out his hand. "I'm Jim Benjamin."

I stood up and as I shook his hand tears came to his eyes. He brushed at them awkwardly with his free hand.

"You'll have to excuse this—happens all the time lately. It's embarrassing." He released my hand and went back to his bunk.

A voice came out of the loudspeaker. "Count time," it said.

By now there was a man at almost every bunk, some sitting, some standing around restlessly.

"They're gonna count our noses," the man in the nearest bunk said in my direction. "Six times a day."

"Okay." Vaguely I remembered that the guard who registered me had told me about the counting system, but I wasn't able to take it all in at the time. Prisoners were counted six times a day—at 12:30, 3:30 and 5:30 A.M. and at 12:30, 4 and 10 P.M. At 4 and 10 P.M. the counts were critical and each man had to be at his bunk. The other four times were treated more casually since most of the inmates were sleeping or working. It just wasn't practical to call the workers back to their dorms when they were working.

A little after 4 o'clock a guard came in and counted the men present. "A and O building, forty-eight," he said into the speaker, and almost immediately a voice answered, "Forty-eight, right." Then the guard left.

The room grew noisy. Several men started for the mess hall, which opened at 4:30. Some stood around in small groups, talking loudly. Radios were turned on full blast. I saw a few men stretched out on their beds, staring at the ceiling, oblivious to the sounds of a rock song coming from a speaker only a few inches from one of their ears. Jim Benjamin was sitting on his bed, his head in his hands, and the man in the bunk next to his sat in a straight-backed wooden chair with one wide arm, staring at the metal cabinet in front of him.

Then I saw someone I recognized coming toward me and smiling—Bud Krogh. I had known he was at Allenwood, but in the strangeness of my first hour there, I had forgotten.

"Jeb," he said, grabbing my hand. "Good to see

you!" Then he caught himself. "Not that it's good to see you *here*. But—you know—"

"Sure," I replied. "I would have said the same thing. In fact, it's *great* to see you. It's a break to see someone I know."

"Well, it won't be for long," Bud informed me. "They're sending me to Fort Holabird tomorrow morning." He read the disappointment in my face. "It's in Baltimore," he explained. "I have to testify in the Ellsberg case and the prosecutors want me nearby." He shrugged. "At least, so they say. Frankly, I don't think they want two Watergate guys in Allenwood."

"We might compare notes, huh?" I asked, and he nodded.

"At least I can show you around," he went on. "We've got six hours till lights out, with nothing else to do."

Bud began by introducing me to some of the men he knew. One of the first was Lou Tonti, who later would be my bunkmate. He was in for extortion. "He ran for governor of New Jersey once," Bud told me. "Used to be head of the New Jersey Highway Authority."

Then Bud took me to another dorm to meet Bill Edwards who worked as a clerk in the Administration Building. Bill had been at Allenwood almost three years and would be out in a few months. "He's a good guy," Bud said. "He knows how to cut the red tape around here."

"Sounds like we're back in politics," I observed.

Suddenly Bud was serious. "I want to tell you something, Jeb, and I hope you remember it, because maybe it'll help. This is a system, same as any other system. If you want to survive, you've got to learn how things work."

"I'm sorry, Bud," I said, knowing I was behaving

strangely, but not being able to do anything about it. "I appreciate what you're doing—except it isn't coming out that way."

"I know. I was the same way when I came in. It's a form of shock, Jeb. It'll take a while to get over it."

Walking down the hill toward the mess hall, which was in the rear of the Administration Building, Bud stopped to introduce me to a few other inmates. I didn't remember their names, but most of them seemed to fit into the "white-collar" classification.

"Actually there aren't very many of us here," Bud said. "In spite of what you've heard about Allenwood, white collars are in the minority. Most of the prisoners are from the ghetto, and there are a few Mafia men."

Then he gave me the same advice Clifford Irving had given me. "They won't bother you as long as you keep to yourself and mind your own business. Don't try to get in with them—they don't want you. That's why I'm pointing out a few men you probably can talk to. Just don't get too friendly with any of them."

Before we came to the door of the administration building, Bud pulled me aside. "I'd better warn you about one thing, Jeb," he said in a low voice. "A lot of these guys are in on drug charges, and they're not going to feel very friendly toward anyone connected with Richard Nixon—the way they look at it, he's the one who put them here."

Bud was talking about the drug abuse laws, which had been stiffened under the Nixon Administration. In fact, while I was on the White House staff Bud had drafted some of the anti-drug legislation that was later passed by Congress. Later, both of us had worked on the implementation of the new drug laws.

"Whatever you do, don't mention that part of your life," Bud warned. "If anyone asks you what you did in the government, tell him you were in public relations."

Though I knew Bud was trying to cram as much advice as possible into the few hours we had together, my mind began to resist the onslaught of information I was receiving. I felt myself withdrawing, hearing the words but not comprehending them. There was a sense of unreality about everything, the way it is when you're dreaming—except that when you're dreaming you usually expect to wake up. I had no such expectation.

The dining room was meant to be attractive. It was a large room with tall windows on one end that looked out on the surrounding hills. Almost all the furniture was plastic, in bright shades of yellow and orange.

We took our trays and went through the line. Although I came away with food on my plate, I don't remember what it was. Nor did I eat any of it. Even if it had been good I don't think I had the appetite for it. Later, when the initial daze had worn off, it didn't seem to make any difference whether I had an appetite. Like most other prisoners, I ate very little, partly because I wasn't hungry and partly because the food was prepared so badly. The menu was heavy on starchy foods; there was a lot of pork and little beef or dairy products—and almost everything was boiled beyond recognition. We could eat as much as we wanted, but few men went back for seconds.

Bud and I sat down at a table across from two young men who said hello to Bud. Again the introductions went around, but I really wasn't listening. Then gradually I began to pull myself out from the mental closet where I had hidden awhile.

Bob Warner, the man sitting across the table

from me, was a Presbyterian minister. He and I had gone to the same school, Williams College, and he was a few years younger. But there the similarity stopped. Warner was in prison for setting fire to an ROTC building on the University of Hawaii campus. He was like the antiwar militants who frequently marched back and forth in front of the White House when I was there.

Peter Tusovitch, the young man sitting next to Warner, was a draft resister. Strange company Bud and I were keeping—but in prison, as I was to learn, individual differences don't matter much. Cultural background is something else.

After we left the mess hall Bud and I took a long walk down to the small frame church at the far end of the prison grounds. He told me there were services every Sunday, one for Catholics and one for Protestants. "They don't amount to much," he said. "In fact, I found them depressing."

In his college days Bud had been a cross-country runner, and as we walked back he gave me a few tips about jogging. "Exercise can save your sanity," he said, "and running is something you can do by yourself. Don't count on the so-called recreational facilities here—the tennis court is a mess. Besides, most of the men who are here for a while don't have the energy to move around. Don't let that happen to you, Jeb. Keep running."

We stopped at Bud's dorm and he gave me a pair of his sweatpants and a pair of sneakers. "I won't need these at Holabird—I'll be getting out in a couple of days." After serving four months and seventeen days of his six-month sentence, Bud was automatically due for release. In such short sentences there is no Parole Board involvement.

Before going back to my dorm we went to the prison commissary. Each prisoner was allowed to spend $40 a month for such things as shaving cream, razor blades, toothpaste, candy, fruit juice, soft drinks, and cigarettes. I had deposited $100 to my account when I entered prison, but it would be a few days before the account was processed and opened. So Bud picked out things he knew I would need and paid for them out of his account, which still had money in it.

Bud also bought me a little Panasonic radio which he said would be good company for me. Back in my dorm he went looking through the unassigned beds until he found a bedboard for me.

"Not all—but some—of the comforts of home," he joked as he helped me put the bedboard under my mattress.

"I'll try to get back to see you in the morning," he promised. Then he left.

That first night I didn't sleep very well. I kept waking up, thinking I was home, and wondering what was so different about my bedroom. Then I would see the light coming in from the lobby outside the dorm where some of the men were watching television. In the half-light I saw the other beds in the room and realized I was in prison. It hadn't been a dream.

During the night, the noise was as constant as the noise you hear on a city street—but instead of horns, screeching tires, and the stopping and starting of vehicles, there were the communal sounds of approximately fifty men housed together and talking, griping, arguing, snoring, and moaning in their sleep. The lights in the dorm went out at 10:15 o'clock after the count, but the lobby was brightly lit and the TV set kept going all night. There was always someone moving back and forth between his bunk and the lobby.

I was awake for the 12:30 and 3:30 counts and saw the guard moving between the rows of beds, occasionally shining his flashlight into the face of a sleeping prisoner. By the next count—it must have been at 5:30—I had dozed off and I woke up to the flashlight in my face. I wondered how anyone slept, yet some of the men seemed to be unconscious. After a while I probably wouldn't notice the noise— the way people who live along the railroad tracks don't notice the passing trains.

The next morning I saw Bud briefly in the mess hall. "Did you get any sleep?" he asked.

"A little," I replied, somewhat surprised that I didn't really feel tired. "I'll be all right—ten months isn't such a long time."

What I said must have bothered Bud. He started to comment, but seemed to change his mind. He took a swallow of coffee and made a face. Then he held the cup in both hands, propped his elbows on the table, and leaned close to me.

"It may be longer than ten months."

"What do you mean? The judge recommended me for parole in ten months."

"Yes, but parole isn't automatic."

"Why not? I'm not planning to get in any trouble. Why shouldn't I get a parole?"

"It just doesn't work that way. Believe me, you've got to be on the inside of a prison to find out how parole works. Lawyers don't know."

Breakfast that morning was chipped beef in a heavy cream sauce on a thick slice of white bread. I pushed the plate away from me.

"Okay, Bud, tell me, how does it work?" I asked.

He realized that I needed to hear the truth from him. "The judge said you should be *eligible* for parole in ten months—that doesn't mean you'll *get* paroled. The Parole Board is completely autonomous.

Nobody can tell those guys what to do—and they have their own ideas about the length of time a man ought to serve. Usually they're a lot tougher than a judge or a jury. They have a list of guidelines—so many years for such and such a crime. Get yourself a copy."

"But doesn't my sentence mean anything?"

"Sure. It means you could be here as long as thirty-two months. You get a certain amount of time off for good behavior, and that's something the Parole Board can't touch. But anything less than that is up to them, and usually they feel a man ought to serve at least a third of his maximum sentence."

"Which could mean sixteen months in my case, right?" I said.

"I'm sorry, Jeb," Bud looked up at the clock and started to get his plates together on his tray. He would be leaving soon. "It could mean even more than sixteen. You never know. They usually want white-collar types to do it all."

In the outside world I wouldn't have been so disturbed over the difference of six months. But even though I hadn't been in Allenwood for twenty-four hours, I sensed that time was going to move very slowly. Six months—even six days more than I had expected seemed endless. And what about Gail and the children? How could I tell them that they would have to be on their own almost twice as long as we had anticipated? Money was only one of the problems they would have.

As I shook hands with Bud before he left and wished him luck, I was thinking about Gail. I couldn't go to her. No matter what happened, I had to stay where I was. That was when I really began to feel the confinement of prison.

I decided to call my lawyers and tell them what

Bud had told me. The camp's only public telephone was in another part of the administration building, and when I got there I saw a line of men outside the booth. One of them told me I had to get permission from my caseworker before I could use the phone.

"Who's my caseworker?" I asked him.

"They'll get around to telling you one of these days," the man said, smiling. It was the kind of smile I was to see often in prison, one that took pleasure in another man's pain and frustration. Not that it expressed sadism; it simply meant that a man felt a little less miserable when he saw someone who felt as bad as or worse than he did.

I saw Bill Edwards coming out of the mess hall and remembered that he worked in administration. With his help I located one of the three prison caseworkers and waited in line outside his office to explain why I wanted to use the phone. It took me almost all day to get permission, and it was late in the afternoon when I got to use the phone. Fortunately, Jim Sharp was in his office.

With so many men waiting to use the phone I didn't want to go into detail about my sentence, so I told Jim I had heard some disturbing news about paroles and asked him if he could come to Allenwood. He said he would be there later that week—and not to worry.

I was beginning to feel very tired, so I went back to my dorm to rest. There wasn't much else for me to do; I hadn't been assigned to a job yet.

The room was almost empty. Jim Benjamin, the only man whose face I could connect with a name, was gone. A few men were stretched out on their beds, sleeping. I wasn't sure, but they seemed to be the same ones who had been sleeping the day before. The man in the bunk next to Jim Benjamin's was sitting in his chair again, writing a letter.

I lay down on my bed, expecting to fall asleep. But I didn't—my eyes were wide open. Reaching into my locker, I took out my Bible, leafing through it to find some of the passages Louie and I had gone over together. For some reason my mind refused to recall chapter and verse numbers and the pages were a blur, so I put the Bible back. Then I saw that the man across the aisle had stopped writing and was staring into space again. I got up and went over to him.

"Excuse me," I said and introduced myself.

He looked at me with no expression on his face. "I know," he replied. Though he didn't tell me his name, it was not because he was hostile. He just didn't seem to think of it.

"I noticed you sitting here yesterday," I went on, feeling a little awkward. "And then today I saw you doing the same thing, just looking up at the wall over there."

"I know," he said. "I was trying to write a letter, but I don't know what to say. I haven't seen my brother for many years. Can't seem to do anything but sit here."

"How about going for a walk? Or watching a little TV?" I invited.

"No. I can't seem to." He shook his head sadly. "I just came down from Lewisburg. I'm getting out in two months."

"That's great," I said.

"No, it isn't," he answered. "I don't know what I'm going to do on the outside. I was in a cell by myself for fifteen years, with nothing to do—all day, all night. I just sat and looked at the wall. Looks like that's about all I know how to do."

I couldn't think of anything reassuring to say to a man like that. The outside world wasn't going to understand him. Two days ago I would have believed that a man, *any* man, could pull himself up by his own bootstraps. But after only a short time in prison, I was beginning to see that when a man spends a certain amount of time alone, with nothing to do but sit and stare, he doesn't have any bootstraps left to pull.

The man was staring again and probably wouldn't have heard me if I had thought of something to say. I put my hand on his shoulder briefly and then went back to my bed.

Since arriving at Allenwood I hadn't tried to pray. I was in too much of a daze to communicate on anything but the most basic earthly levels. But, lying on my bed, knowing that I would never lose the mental picture of that man sitting in his chair, I did not feel that I was alone. Christ was with me in that prison. I had felt his presence all along, and I thought I understood his silence. He was waiting for the initial shock of confinement to wear off. But because he was there, I knew I wasn't going to end up staring at the wall.

Not that being a Christian would make my prison term easy for me. Jesus wasn't going to spare me the pain, or the problems that were the natural consequences of life. But he was going to give me enough strength to endure the pain, and he would help me find ways to work out my problems. He would meet me *in* the pain. Like everyone else who goes to prison, I would become depressed; being a Christian didn't exempt me from that experience. I was going to miss my wife and my children and my friends, and I would feel lonelier than I ever had in my entire life. I was going to become even more aware of the hurt I had brought to those I loved, and I would know the helplessness of being unable to comfort them. But he was there with me. That was going to make the difference.

6

View from the Inside

MOST OF THE MEN in Allenwood were in far worse condition then I was. And if Jesus Christ had not been in control of my life, I would probably have dismissed their plight with something like: "Well, they've got it rough—but what can I do about it?"

But Christ wouldn't let me get away with that kind of an attitude. He broke me wide open.

For most of my time in prison I lived like any other inmate: concerned for my own survival. And that is a legitimate concern, because not everyone does survive. There are so many ways a man can be destroyed. He can become mentally unbalanced; he can be physically abused, even murdered, by other prisoners; he can become so depressed that he loses all initiative; or he can become bitter about what is happening to him. So the struggle to survive is a necessary one. But in the struggle a man can become so self-centered that no one else matters. I was headed in that direction, but Christ kept me from going all the way.

As Louie Evans had explained to me, becoming a Christian made me more sensitive to the feelings of those around me. And in prison I was surrounded by "human vibrations."

There is no way a person taking a tour of a prison can understand what prison really is, because it isn't something you can see. Forget the buildings, however well equipped they may be—and believe me, in many penal institutions they are not. Forget the bars on the windows or the watchtowers or the cells. None of these things makes a prison, because prison is a state of mind. It is a loss of freedom, which isn't a simple matter of someone telling you where you can and can't go. It means that you are totally removed from the world you knew, and that world has to get along without you and you without it—clumsily at first, perhaps, but eventually as well as if you had never existed. Whatever you do and whoever you are, you have no effect on the world. Your footprints are washed away and you begin to wonder whether you ever did exist. You can't find any evidence that anyone cares whether you exist now. That's when you start losing your identity as a human being.

A few of us were lucky. We were educated. Since we had encountered "the system" before in our jobs, after a few weeks we were able to figure out how the system worked in prison. Finding out where the red tape was and how to get around it kept our frustration to a minimum. We had never expected to be in prison, and most likely we wouldn't be returning after we got out. Our families gave us support, and we knew they were waiting for us to come home. Prison was a temporary state of mind.

But the more typical prisoner is a person who has never had the advantages that the average white, middle-class American takes for granted. He comes from the ghetto; he dropped out of school as soon as he could because he wasn't getting anything out of it anyway; he can barely read and write; and he never had a real job. He's been in prison before and he'll be back again not long after he gets out. Crime is the only way to survive that he knows.

Most of the blacks and Spanish-speaking men were like this typical prisoner. In one sense they didn't suffer the shock of adjusting to prison life, but only because so many of them had been there before. Instead of a system that they could compare with other organized institutions they had known, prison to them was an overwhelming, mindless thing. It constantly found ways to frustrate them and remind them that they were not human.

From day to day the rules changed. One day you were told your visitors could bring you food, but by the time your visitors arrived the rules were changed and no food of any kind was allowed. Your visitors had to be approved in advance and sometimes you didn't get the approval until the very last minute. Then it was too late to get in touch with anyone you wanted to see. After ninety days in prison you were eligible for a weekend with your family, subject to approval—and that approval sometimes didn't come in time for you to make any arrangements with your wife and children.

It was especially hard for a man in prison to deal with family emergencies. The wives of most of the married prisoners were on welfare. At times they

were desperate for another place to live because
their apartment building had been condemned.
Sometimes a child, a wife, a mother, or a father became critically ill, and the man in prison almost
went out of his mind sitting in the caseworker's
crowded outer office, waiting for an interview and a
chance to explain why he had to go home to
straighten things out. According to the rules in a
minimum security prison, a man could be granted
emergency leave in such cases. But the rules could
be interpreted differently by a caseworker who was
convinced that every prisoner was trying to con him.
Often the decision was "No. Leave denied."

It happened to Bill Edwards a few weeks after I
came to Allenwood. His ex-wife had remarried, and
her new husband had beaten her and Bill's little
boy. She wrote to Bill from the hospital, asking him
to help her find a place where the boy could be safe
until she had a chance to recover and straighten out
her life. Bill applied for emergency leave, and when
he didn't get it he seriously thought of "going over
the hill."

"I'll come back," he promised.

A few of us were trying to change his mind.
"You're almost out of here," we told him. "You
take a walk and they'll add six months to your sentence."

"I gotta help my kid," he insisted. How he was
going to do that, we couldn't imagine. His only rela-
tive was a married sister who evidently didn't need
any more problems.

"Wait," we said to him. "Give us a few days to
come up with an idea—okay?"

It was hard for Bill to say yes because he didn't
believe in anything—he had no hope. But he agreed.
Still, we could see he didn't expect results, and we
knew he was already trying to decide what time of

day would be best for getting out of there.

Lou Tonti, a few other men, and I started getting in line at the phone booth, calling anyone we thought might be able to take Bill's boy. But an abused child from a broken home, whose father was in prison, wasn't exactly easy to place. Then Gail had an idea. She called Bud and Sue Krogh. Bud had just come home from prison, and he and Sue had their own problems, but they said they could take care of the boy, at least for a while.

Bill wasn't the kind to show surprise, but he couldn't hide the relief he must have felt. Of course it went against his philosophy that nothing ever went right for him.

"Now you've got to work on your sister and get her to take the boy until you get out," Lou suggested.

"She'll never do that," Bill replied.

"Try," Lou insisted.

"Okay." For Bill, that was a lot. Fortunately, his sister later agreed to take the boy, which solved the problem at least temporarily.

I was right. The inmates who had been sleeping that first day were still sleeping the next day. That was all they ever seemed to do. I never saw them in the mess hall, in the lobby, or on their way to a job. One of them I never saw upright; we used to call him "El Prono." And there I was, having trouble getting any sleep at all.

After a while I discovered that many prisoners took some form of tranquilizer to make them sleep. It was easier to get something like that than to make a phone call. All a man had to do was say he couldn't sleep and he got all the tranquilizers he wanted. So some men took them all the time and stayed in bed, which was their way of cheating the government out of the time they were spending in prison. The guards seemed to feel it was less trouble to let them sleep than to hassle them into getting up.

I wanted to hold out, but I couldn't. Loss of sleep was wearing me down and threatening me with more depression than I could handle. Finally I asked for a tranquilizer, and after one good night's sleep I felt so much better that I took one pill a night for the next few weeks.

"Watch out for anyone who's mentally unbalanced," Bud had warned me. "There's a lot of that here." After a few weeks I could see that he wasn't exaggerating. Some of the men obviously should have been sent to mental institutions rather than to prison. For some others, prison itself was the thing that drove them over the edge. I tried to keep my distance from anyone in either category.

Violence wasn't expected in a prison like Allenwood, but it always lay just below the surface and occasionally it erupted. Thrown in with an inmate population whose crimes were basically nonviolent was a small group of men who were sent down from Lewisburg to spend the last few months of their sentence in a less restrictive atmosphere. They weren't many, but their presence was disturbing. Most of them had been convicted of violent crimes such as rape, assault, manslaughter, and armed robbery, and they had spent years in an institution where survival was much more difficult. It was the assumption of the penal authorities that these men would stay out of trouble in Allenwood because they would not want to jeopardize their chance of getting out. Most of the time that assumption was correct. But they were the "tough guys," and they wanted the rest of us to remember that.

Almost paranoid in their suspicion that someone was out to get them, the "tough guys" had brutal ways of settling their scores. Most of them carried some kind of a knife or sharp instrument, which they actually had needed for their own protection in Lewisburg. To the rest of us who were unarmed, and wouldn't have known how to handle a weapon if we had one, it was like being in the same room with someone carrying a concealed H-bomb. A few weeks after I arrived, there was a stabbing. Then one night a prisoner was badly beaten about the head with a heavy combination lock wrapped in a sock. Assailants unknown.

Even without the men from Lewisburg there would have been the threat of violence. No one is happy in prison—unless he is truly insane—and bitterness is almost inevitable. Put enough bitter men together and you're going to have arguments, scuffles, and a few punches thrown.

Racial tensions were always present, although they weren't always serious. Many of the prisoners were black, and as far as they were concerned, whites were the ones who put them in prison. The smaller number of white inmates only seemed to confirm that view. After I saw what deprivation and inequality of opportunity had done to the blacks, I couldn't disagree with them.

Usually the blacks taunted the white prisoners with remarks like: "I didn't think they let any of you guys in prison," or "Hey, whitey, I thought you were the big man out there—how'd you end up in here with us?" But they were spoken half-seriously, half-jokingly, and if you didn't let the remarks get under your skin, you didn't have any trouble.

Then a few weeks later a group of prisoners came down from Danbury penitentiary, which was overcrowded at the time. These men weren't like the Lewisburg men; they weren't about to get out, and being among so many men with shorter sentences was painfully frustrating. They were openly hostile, and the tensions between blacks and whites increased as the Allenwood blacks began looking to the Danbury blacks as their leaders. There was no more joking; now there were threats. The guards ignored the situation, which meant that the white prisoners were on their own.

It could have been serious, except that Johnny Sample arrived at exactly the right moment. He was the kind of man the black prisoners needed: a former pro football star for the New York Jets, he was outgoing, outspoken, and a very nice guy, a natural hero. I'll never know how he got mixed up in a bad-check charge, but I really didn't care. Neither did anyone else. Johnny had energy and he liked to organize things.

I had moved into my permanent dorm when Johnny came in, and we found we both liked to play tennis. The court was lumpy, the tapes were gone, and the net was pathetic, but usually the few people who played tennis made the best of it. Not Johnny.

"It's a mess," he said shading his eyes from the sun and squinting in disgust. "How can you play on this?"

"Not very well," I replied. "But it's exercise."

"When I play, I want to *play*," he went on.

"Well, maybe we can fix it up," I suggested. "Tape can't cost that much."

The tape cost a bit more than we expected, but it was worth every cent. We got permission for Gail to bring in the tape on one of her visits, and Johnny and I nailed it down. We smoothed the court and repaired the net. When we finally were able to play a decent game, it gave us a special satisfaction.

Johnny had many admirers who used to stand around the tennis court, watching us play. Ordinarily they probably would have given the players a hard time, but they respected Johnny and watched silently.

While we were fixing the court, we played tennis on the indoor basketball court, which was better than nothing. As usual, wherever Johnny went, he was followed by a group of other inmates, and they would watch us play. Soon it became obvious that these men wanted to play, too, but didn't know what tennis was all about. So I offered to teach them—which is how I became the Allenwood tennis pro. Every Tuesday and Thursday nights I gave lessons. The men learned fast and seemed to enjoy the game, and it gave me something to look forward to.

By far the biggest problem for any man in Allenwood—as it is in any prison—was depression. It came on you slowly, so that you didn't really see it for what it was. First you found it hard to get up in the morning. It didn't matter whether or not you had slept well the night before; there just was no incentive to get out of bed. One day was as monotonous as the next. Maybe you had a job to do, but it was dull and meaningless and no one seemed to care whether you did it well, or at all. With your appetite gone, you didn't get enough nutrients to replenish your energy, and gradually you became so listless that the slightest bit of effort was more than you could exert. You cried easily, usually without knowing why.

Jim Benjamin was the one I worried about most. He had been in prison twenty-three days when I came to Allenwood, and the reason I knew the exact number of days is that he was so painfully aware of them. Jim had had an especially bad break because he was sent to prison on the day he was sentenced, which would be a shock to anyone. It was more so for him and his family because they didn't expect him to go to prison at all.

Jim had been a doctor with a large practice. He had been convicted of Medicare fraud in a trial that attracted a lot of publicity. Billed as the "Robin Hood doctor," he stole from rich Uncle Sam so he could treat the poor for next to nothing. Because many of his patients came to his defense, Jim thought he probably would be put on probation and possibly fined. It had happened to other doctors who had done the same thing. But instead, Jim got two years, "beginning immediately," and he didn't even have time to go home and say good-by to his four children. His wife was there in court with him, but she was too stunned to realize what was happening when the bailiff led her husband away. I used to see her sometimes when she came to visit Jim, and she still wasn't over the shock.

It didn't help Jim when he was assigned to mowing the warden's lawn. He was a doctor, and Allenwood didn't even have a doctor. How much better it would have been if he could have had a job that would use his professional training and experience and at the same time serve the prisoners' medical needs without any expense to the taxpayer.

At times it seemed as if the purpose of prison was to convince a man of his own worthlessness, which, when you thought about it, was a dirty trick to play upon the society that each man eventually would reenter. But when you thought about it some more, you realized that probably it wasn't deliberate—because there really didn't seem to be a purpose or policy of any kind in prison. As Karl Menninger put it in *The Crime of Punishment,* the function of most prisons is to serve as a "warehouse for human beings."

Warehousing was something Doc Benjamin just couldn't accept. After six weeks in Allenwood he still couldn't believe he was there. The sudden tears

I had seen that first day came more often, especially after visits from his wife. Doc also was worried about his teenage children, who were reacting to the shock of his imprisonment with rebellion and defiance. His worry was contagious. I wondered how my oldest boy, Whit, would take the strain.

There wasn't much that I or anyone could do for Doc. He was so exhausted emotionally that he was short-tempered with people, and many prisoners didn't get along with him at all because of this. But a few of us tried to lift him up when he was in particularly low spirits. Actually I probably spent more time with Doc than any of the other prisoners.

Then one morning he came over to my bunk and stood there with his hands in his pockets, shaking his head slowly. "I don't know what to do, Jeb," he muttered.

"What's the matter?" I asked.

"I can't stay here. I just *can't* stay here." For a moment I thought he was thinking of going over the hill. "Don't add to your sentence, Doc," I urged.

"No, no, no—not that kind of thing," he replied. "But I can't stay here. I have to get out."

"How?" I didn't like the look in his eyes.

"I've been thinking, Jeb, and there doesn't seem to be any other way. I might have to kill myself."

I could feel the words coming almost before he spoke them. He was the most desperate, unhappy man I had ever seen. "Don't, Doc," I begged him. "Don't let yourself get pushed that far—think about your wife and your kids."

"I do, all the time," he blurted, and tears came to his eyes. "That's why I can't stay here." He went back to his bunk and lay face down on it. Finally I convinced him to go for a walk down to the church with me, and after we talked for a couple of hours he seemed to feel much better. We could lean on each other, but neither one of us had enough emotional strength to hold the other up. We were lacking the same thing: strokes.

It was the psychologist Eric Berne who started people thinking in terms of "strokes" when he did his pioneering work in transactional analysis. I remember reading his statement that an infant who was otherwise well cared for would die if he didn't receive any attention and affection, and it seemed to me that that was what caused so much depression in prison. We were well cared for physically—that is, we weren't like Alexander Solzhenitsyn, freezing and starving in a Siberian prison. But there was no kindness, no caring about us as human beings, no understanding of what we were feeling—no strokes. And because of that, the prisoners did strange things. Jim Benjamin was trying to die.

Some men turned to each other. I had heard about homosexuality in prison, and it was evident in Allenwood. But it wasn't forced on young, attractive prisoners in Allenwood (the way it was in maximum security institutions). In Allenwood, the relationship was consentual, and many men who had never participated in homosexual activities before were caught up in them. I don't think most of the men considered themselves "deviant." It just seemed to me that they were reaching out for whatever affection was available to them. Maybe they were dying for the lack of it. Most of them belonged to that majority of inmates who had been abandoned by their families and friends, and who never had visitors or received any mail.

Depression caused many prisoners to neglect their appearance. You could get your khakis pressed if you knew someone who worked in the laundry and needed something you were willing to swap—such as cigarettes (which in my case were as good as gold because I don't smoke). But if a man didn't think anyone cared how he looked, he wore his khakis wrinkled, and he seldom shaved. If it hadn't been for Gail and the children coming to see me every week, I would have looked much worse.

Every other month you would notice some of the men pulling themselves together, getting their clothes pressed and putting a shine on their shoes. They would shave daily and get a haircut. They put their bunks in order and cleared the junk off the tops of their cabinets. Even those who seemed to do nothing but sleep sat up on the edge of their beds, focusing their eyes and stretching. The signs were unmistakable: it was Parole Board time.

The Philadelphia office of the Parole Board sent examiners to Allenwood every two months to interview prisoners who were eligible for parole. The examiners, who were civil servants, went over a man's records before speaking to him. Considering the amount of time the examiners spent at the prison and the number of prisoners they had to review, I doubt that they had more than a few minutes to give to each case. That's hardly enough time to get to know a man and evaluate his future potential, but it seemed to me that the Parole Board wasn't really interested in evaluating. Their concern was whether the man had been punished enough, in their view, for what he had done.

Never having had to go before a Parole Board examiner, I can't speak about the experience firsthand. I can only describe the reactions I saw in some of the inmates.

A prisoner who was eligible for parole had to fill out a long application form and give it to a caseworker, who sent it on to the Board. But right there in the initial stages there was a catch: an unbelievable number of prisoners didn't know how to fill out a form properly, and if they did anything wrong, or left a blank unfilled, no one explained how to correct the error. The form was simply returned to them; it could bounce back and forth between prisoner and caseworker forever. And as long as there was no completed form, there was no interview.

If there's one thing a white-collar man knows how to do, it's fill out an application. I could do it in my sleep because it had been as much a part of my life as brushing my teeth before going to bed. It was one of the few things I was able to do for another prisoner, which made my life there a little less futile. If I had been a lawyer I could have done much more. So many of the inmates had received the services of public defenders in their court appearances, and in most cases those services ended the moment the convicted man went to prison.

Cornelius Gallagher, a former congressman from New Jersey who was in on a bribery conviction, came up for parole while I was in Allenwood. Of course, he had no trouble with the application form, but he ran into another unexpected obstacle which the Parole Board seemed to feel obligated to put between a man and his freedom.

Neal looked pretty sharp the day he was supposed to see the examiner. A few days earlier he had been pessimistic about the outcome because this was his last chance for parole and, as Bud had warned me, the Board usually didn't approve of short sentences for white-collar prisoners. Neal had been sentenced to two years, and in such cases the Board usually made a man do it all because they felt the sentence was too short. But as the day of the appointment for the interview came closer, Neal became more and more optimistic. "Wish me luck," he said, waving, as I passed him that day.

Later he stopped by my dorm, looking more dejected than ever. "What do you think?" he growled angrily.

I just looked at him.

"I was convicted on one charge, and sentenced according to that one charge—right?" he asked. "Now, all of a sudden, other charges that were only *considered* before the trial have something to do with my sentence."

"What do you mean?" I asked. I recalled that at the time I went to the prosecutors, they also were considering a charge of perjury, but they changed their minds. Legally, that charge wasn't part of my case.

"Anything anybody ever *thought* you might have done is important to the Parole Board. What you were tried for doesn't mean a thing. The way they look at it, maybe you also did such-and-such, and such-and-such, so that makes you a pretty bad character. They want to be sure you pay a big enough debt to society."

"Can they do that?" I asked.

"Sure!" he retorted. "Parole boards are autonomous."

"They turned you down?" I continued.

"You can bet on it," Neal answered. "They don't let you know for a few weeks, but I could tell from the examiner's attitude, and the questions he asked. Don't expect to get out for a long time, Magruder."

I didn't think Neal was exaggerating because his experience was repeated in several other men who saw the Parole Board examiner at that time. But Neal was more articulate, and angry as he was, he was able to get his feelings out in the open. Some of the other inmates—not being able to size up the system—took the rejection as one more door slammed in their faces, with no reason given. The anger they must have felt couldn't be directed at its source, but it would come to the surface in some way at another time, or it would drive them deeper into depression.

The chances for parole was The Topic of Conversation in Allenwood, and from all I've heard, it is true of prisons in general. It brought out the "I'm not okay, but you're even *less* okay than I am" in almost everyone. Like the funny smile I had seen on a man that first day, it made a prisoner's inner pain throb just a little less if he could make himself think another man's pain was worse. At first it shook me up. A man would turn to me and ask, "How long did you say you got sent up for?"

And I'd reply, "Ten months to four years."

"Oh, man!" he'd answer, slapping his palm to his forehead or rolling his eyes toward the ceiling. "Ten months to—and *how* long do you think you'll be here?"

"Well, I'm hoping ten months. That's when I'm eligible for parole."

"Forget it!" he'd go on. "They'll never let you out that early. They'll want to make an example of you guys—you're gonna max out."

"Max out" means that a man serves the full amount of his sentence, minus time allowed for good behavior. To max out, in my case, would have meant serving thirty-two months, or two-thirds of the maximum part of my sentence.

After a while I began to realize that this was a game prisoners played with each other. Nevertheless, it was uncomfortably close to reality. When I read a copy of the Parole Board guidelines, I saw that for each type of crime, a certain length of sentence was specified. It didn't matter whether a man had been sentenced by a "tough" judge or an "easy" one, because the Parole Board had its own ideas about what kind of punishment fit the crime. Neither did good behavior influence their decisions, from what I could see, because model prisoners were turned down as easily as anyone else.

So, to most prisoners, going before the Parole Board was like being tried all over again. And when a man's request for parole was rejected, it was like being sentenced all over again. Still, a man couldn't help but hope that in his case it might be different. I knew I would do the same when my turn came.

I already knew how the system worked at the top; now I was finding out how it worked at the bottom. There really isn't much difference.

In Washington and in the business world, if you want to get things done, you have to learn who makes the wheels turn, and it isn't always the person whose name is lettered on the door. Often it is the secretary or the administrative assistant. In prison it was the same.

At first I wasted a lot of time waiting to see a caseworker. Every visitor had to be approved, as well as anything a visitor brought in, so that when Gail wanted to give me a set of oil paints she couldn't just hand the box over to me. I had to see the caseworker and try to get permission. Most of the time the answer was no, which, if you looked at it from the caseworker's point of view, was a little easier than saying yes because that ended the matter and didn't require any paperwork. Once I realized that there was no rationale behind the negative answer—other than the caseworker's convenience—I began to suspect that I was going about things in the wrong way. Bill Edwards confirmed my suspicion.

"See the clerk who works for the caseworker," Bill said. "He runs the office."

The clerk was an inmate who seemed like a capable guy. I had seen other inmates walk into the caseworker's office, go straight to the clerk, hand him a form, and walk away with it initialed. Actually the clerk had written the caseworker's initials and his own, meaning that he had okayed the form in the caseworker's absence. And that, in any bureaucracy, is as good as the required signature.

The next time I wanted to add a name to my visitor list, I took the shortcut and went to the clerk. In two minutes flat I came away with the approval I needed.

Gradually I realized that the prisoners ran everything. During my first three weeks at Allenwood I was assigned to kitchen duty. In fact, I was the only prisoner in the A & O dorm who was given any kind of work to do, and I had the feeling that the warden wanted to show the other inmates that I wasn't getting any special treatment. To emphasize the point I was given the grubbiest kind of kitchen duty—scrubbing the pots and pans. The water was hot, and I was always enveloped in steam. But actually I welcomed the work because it gave me something to do.

One day I was working in the butcher department and noticed an inmate setting aside some beautiful cuts of meat that had just been delivered. Having eaten the prison food, I was sure we never got meat like that.

"Why are you putting these aside?" I asked the inmate.

"That's for the guards to take home," he replied. "I do it all the time." Then when he saw the puzzled look on my face he went on, "What else can I do? If I say no, those guys will make life miserable for me. Maybe you think I should go tell the warden his guards are rippin' off half his meat, huh? A lot he cares!"

It was ironic that men who were supposed to be

protecting society from criminals like us were stealing the food out of our mouths. But meat was only
one of the things that had a way of disappearing.

I was taken off kitchen duty to replace a clerical
worker in the foreman's office who was getting paroled. As my predecessor was explaining how the
supplies and equipment were to be recorded as they
came in and were used, he said, "There's always a
discrepancy in the gasoline. The figures won't
tally."

"Why not?" I asked.

"Because we don't record every gallon we give
out, that's why," he retorted, and I knew he wanted
to add the word "Stupid."

I probably egged him on by asking "Why not?"
again.

He sighed. "A lot of the gas in those pumps
doesn't even get to the farm machinery. It goes into
private cars—the guards', the administrators'—you
get the idea."

"Okay," I said, "so there's a discrepancy."

"That's just what I'm trying to tell you—there
can't be any discrepancy. You have to juggle the
figures."

"Oh, no," I denied. "*You* juggle them if you want
to, that's your business. But I've already had my
cover-up."

By the time I made up my first report the clerk
was gone, and I don't know what happened to the
discrepancy, which was quite large. I let it stand in
the report. Perhaps someone else fooled with the figures—or maybe a discrepancy didn't mean anything
to the higher-ups in Lewisburg. Maybe they saw too
many of them, because I'm sure there were other
ways in which some of the guards and administrative personnel were stealing from the system. They
were like the man who sticks a stapling machine

into his briefcase when no one is looking because, well, the company can afford it.

But to a prisoner from the ghetto the hypocrisy of the guards only confirmed his belief that there are two classes of people in this life: those who get caught and those who get away with it, and he had no doubt about which category he fit into. Could you blame him for feeling that the system was rigged against him when he was serving time for doing something his guards were doing right in front of his eyes?

That's why the night of 8 August 1974 had a special significance for many of the men in Allenwood —and, I'm sure, in prisons all over the country. It had a special significance for me, too, but in a different way.

Everyone was watching TV that night, waiting for the President of the United States to tell his fellow citizens that he was going to resign. For me it was almost impossible to believe that only two years ago, he—and everyone around him—was rolling toward the most decisive election victory in history, a mandate big enough to bring tears to a man's eyes. And then there was the familiar face on the television screen, only haggard and tormented now, and the brief announcement that it was all over—the victory, the mandate, and the man himself.

As the President ended his message, the room suddenly vibrated with cheers, boos, and screeching whistles. Men stomped their feet on the floor and slapped each other on the back. I was shaken out of my sadness by the realization of what Richard Nixon's resignation meant to many of these prisoners. He had been the "law-and-order" candidate, the man who wanted to rid the country of crime by getting tough with criminals. He had been the one who pointed a finger at them, and now he was the one pointed at. The way they looked at it, they had been right all along: there were no good guys. There were only guys who didn't get caught. And, sometimes, only sometimes, one of those was caught, too.

In time I was able to pick up a book and read again, and that helped. Louie Evans sent me several Bible study guides, and when he came to visit me we talked about some of the things I was reading. Even though I had many leisure hours, my attention span was short, so I was making slow progress. But at least the daze was wearing off.

A thought kept passing through my mind. If Watergate hadn't detoured me, I probably never would have become aware of the spiritual starvation I saw in many of the men around me. Because of the crimes that had put them there, prison was even more a state of *soul* than a state of mind, and even when the men got out of Allenwood they would take it with them.

Now I couldn't shrug them off by observing, "That's tough, but what can I do about it?" Somehow I felt that their lives and mine were related, perhaps had always been, and that being in prison was giving me the opportunity to discover that relationship. Not that Watergate happened just to get me into prison. I didn't believe that for one minute. But I felt Jesus Christ beginning to move around through the debris of my former life, sorting out what could be used and what ought to be discarded. Eventually he would let me know what he wanted me to do with the pieces. And one of them would have something to do with prison.

7

Letters from Home

Dear Dad

I howp thet you have a good time at the jail. I and Andy have mayd a club in the atick. The club membs are Andy, Ted, peter, Beaube.

Love

Stu

OOOOOOOOOOOOOOOOOOOOOOOOOOO

XXXXXXXXXXXXXXXXXXXXXXXXXX

OOOOOOOOOOOOOOOOOOOOOOOOOOO

XXXXXXXXXXXXXXXXXXXXXXXXXX

OOOOOOOOOOOOOOOOOOOOOOOOOOO

XXXXXXXXXXXXXXXXXXXXXXXXXX

THIS LETTER FROM my six–year–old son arrived in time for Father's Day, which came shortly after I went to prison. So I was not entirely without "strokes."

Gail visited me most weekends and almost always brought the children with her. We had considered carefully the advisability of allowing the children to come to the prison and finally decided it was better for them to see it for what it was than to imagine it as being far worse. They handled the experience very well, and I think it helped them to understand that although I was separated from them, I had not abandoned them.

In some ways the visits were hard for all of us. I worried about Gail driving four hours each way on narrow roads, and as much as she tried to hide it, I could see how tired she was. Good-bys were difficult, especially for Stuart who could not understand why they had to be. But it was these visits, more than anything else, that kept me from feeling as if my footsteps had been erased from the life I knew. I was still a husband and a father, and we were still a family.

In my daughter's first letter to me she confided: "At night sometimes I cry, and do not worry because we all love you." Even though I also cried over this acknowledgment of her loneliness, I was grateful that she felt close enough to me, in spite of the physical distance between us, to tell me about it. A few weeks later, when she was unable to accompany Gail one Friday, she sent me this note instead:

Dear Dad,
   How are you? I'm fine and doing well. I wish I was going up with Mom tomorrow to see you.
   I'm going to start piano next week. I hope I will play *The Performer* by the Sting and the waltz witch is not by the Sting. Miss Crescent is now Mrs. Gendel but she souns the same.

Dinese has a heat attag but proble will not diy.

When you opon this letter did you notest the smell. This stationery is scented, that is why I used it just for you.

Love and kiss,
Tracy
xxxxxx
oooooo
xxxxxx
oooooo

P.S. Sorry I wote slopy.

Tracy would be all right. She was adjusting to the separation as an unhappy part of a life that otherwise had its good moments.

I could see what was happening. Like me, my family was not being spared the blows of life, but they were getting the help they needed to deal with what was happening to them.

I had worried about Whit and Justin, who were at the age where the approval of their peers was extremely important to them. It was impossible to predict how my prison sentence might affect their relationship with their friends.

Thanks to the decency and intelligence of the masters at St. Alban's School, which both Whit and Justin attended, the boys' acceptance by the other students did not change. I'm sure that was partly due to a thoughtful, inspiring letter written by the Headmaster, Canon Charles Martin, to all the students on the day after the Nixon resignation—and just before school reopened:

Constantly in my thoughts last evening was a visit I had just before school closed with a family deeply involved in Watergate.... The next morning I went to Chapel and tried to order my thoughts so that I could pray. Slowly it became clear to me that whatever the pain to the man and his family, justice had to be done and it was right that it should be done. I was glad that it was being done, but it was also clear that it was not for me to condemn. . . .

In the quiet of the Chapel I knew that wherever we are, whatever we do, there is God. He is in persons, in events, in nature, in all life. In Him we can know the right and find the strength to do the right. I prayed that the Watergate family might find among their friends and in that family which is called the Church that Presence which sustains and enables good to come out of even the deepest of tragedy.

Whit's friendship with Jim Evans was leading him into a deeper awareness of his faith. He was enjoying the Junior High meetings very much. Chuck Reinhold, the Youth Minister at National Presbyterian Church, had been a Young Life worker and seemed to have a special sensitivity to the spiritual needs of young people. He and Whitney got along so well that Whit felt he could turn to Chuck at those times when he needed a father and couldn't wait until visiting day.

As tired as Gail was physically and emotionally, I could see her growing spiritually. She was attending Bible Study Fellowship lectures whenever she could, and she brought her notes along with her when she came to visit so I could share the course with her. Her covenant group was giving her the strength to meet life one day at a time and get through it without cracking up. She could count on their love and support even in the most practical ways, no matter what happened. She could talk to them in complete trust. In the way they cared about her, they were saying, although not in so many words, "This is how Christ loves you, Gail."

Louie Evans came to see me several times. So did my covenant brothers, one at a time. It wasn't the same, talking to them in the nervous atmosphere of the visitors' room, and often after they left, I would remember things I had wanted to say and somehow forgot. But they were there, and that's what counted. So were other friends—Gilly and Joan Gillespie from home, Didi and Harry Riegers from Philadelphia, Rob and Lydia Odle and Bob and Dolores Morgan, who had worked on the campaign with me, Peter Mackey, one of our ministers when we lived in Los Angeles, and his wife Nancy. Bob Frank, another good friend who bought the media advertising in the campaign, put us in touch with the Barlows and the O'Briens, two warm and generous families who lived in the Allenwood area and had Gail and the children stay with them on weekends. Then there were my three clients who had made it possible for me to run a business while I was waiting to be sentenced. Those who couldn't come to Allenwood wrote to me, and before long I was receiving about fifteen letters a day.

Almost every visitor brought me a book, and I had what was probably the best library in the camp, about sixty books and many of them new. I read as much as I could every day, balancing the heavier theological studies with lighter inspirational books. The more groundwork I did in the commentaries, the more I gained from reading the Bible. But I had the feeling that much of what I was reading wasn't staying with me. Depression had reduced my receptivity to anything intellectual because I couldn't identify with the abstract. I was very little thought and all emotions at that point in my life. What I needed was Christ in a flesh–and–blood form, someone I could see and touch, someone who would listen and talk—a rare thing in any part of the world and hardly to be expected in a prison. And yet Christ did come in that way many times—in the family and friends who visited, in the letter writers and message senders. And in the humble, unspectacular, often forgotten men and women whose ministry is the prison.

The spiritual needs of the inmates were almost totally overlooked by the prison authorities. Once a week, usually on Sunday afternoon, the Lewisburg chaplain stopped in, but not for long, because few men asked to see him. He was a grim man who kept himself at a distance and was perhaps too much a victim of the prison itself to be of real help to anyone else. You couldn't blame him for being that way, not when you realized how much time he spent inside prison walls. Even the guards seemed to suffer from the same isolation as the inmates; going home at night wasn't enough to counteract the overall depression.

And so our spiritual needs were met by men and women from *outside* the prison who took Christ seriously when he said, "I was in prison, and ye visited me. . . ."

Every Sunday morning there was a religious service in the small, old, frame church (it was part of a community that had once existed before the land was bought by the federal government). It wasn't much of a service, as services go, and neither was it well attended. Out of almost four hundred inmates, only about ten or fifteen came to church regularly; some of them admittedly came only for a change of scene. We sat in small groups, or alone, quite far apart from each other. During the sermon some of the black members of the congregation murmured "Amen" occasionally. The white parishioners, typically, sat still and said nothing.

The Rev. Mr. Reid, a retired Presbyterian minister, read from the Bible and delivered the sermon. His wife played a few hymns on the piano. They were quiet people and you had the feeling that they cared. Neither seemed to expect anything from the unresponsive prisoners; still, they came to give what they could.

One night a week the men from Yokefellows came into the prison and met with some of us in groups of twelve, a number purposely reminiscent of the disciples and suggested by D. Elton Trueblood, the founder of Yokefellows. These meetings were popular with the prisoners, and many came not because they were Christians but because it helped to be able to talk about problems and look for ways to do something about them. The problems centered around the one big question: "What am I going to do with my life after I get out?" Many of the prisoners really wanted to go straight.

Every Sunday afternoon some of the Yokefellows took a group of prisoners to a local church picnic or dinner. I'm sure they realized that some of the inmates attended the weekly meetings just to get out on an occasional Sunday afternoon, but there was no sign of disapproval or impatience from them. Quite the opposite. Their ministry was genuine: they saw all of us as men created by God and very much in need of his redeeming love—as (and they made this clear) were they.

One Saturday I was in a group taken on a Yokefellow retreat. We went to a camp not far away and spent the day talking about the difficulties we were having in our relationships with our families, our friends, other inmates, and prison officials. It wasn't a rap session, but a good opportunity to let out much of the frustration building up inside us. It helped us to look at our behavior patterns more objectively. No one said, "Well, now, this is how a Christian ought to deal with that situation," which probably would have lost more attention than it gained. The advice and suggestions were practical and sympathetic; they were based on the kind of things Christ might have done in a particular situation. It was valuable experience and stayed with me for a long time.

A small group of four—two men in on drug charges, a bank robber and I—began meeting occasionally in the evenings to pray and talk about the meaning of Christ in our lives. Our religious experiences had been different, and we were in different stages of spiritual maturity, but we had one thing in common: we had lives to rebuild and we wanted Christ to be at the core of them. So we spent most of our time together discussing the practical problems we would face after prison, and in our prayers we asked God to guide us toward solutions that would reflect his will for each of us.

Originally our group had intended to concentrate on reading the Bible together, but the other men were having the same difficulty I was in concentrating on the abstract. Our crucial need, at that time, was for the fellowship of other Christians—and this was what we gave each other. We knew we didn't have to fear one another—a rare experience in prison where everyone is afraid most of the time. We could talk about our faith, our hopes and fears in complete trust, knowing we were constantly in the prayers of the others, and we could experience the presence of Christ among us.

These fleeting, sometimes anxious relationships were beginning to convey something to me. I realized that the system—which can be found almost anywhere in our society—is an elitist structure based upon the achievement of power. If you want to be part of the system, you have to want some of that power and do everything you can to get it.

People without power are considered failures, and, worse than that, nonhuman creatures whose lives and needs should be ignored; they may as well not have any needs as far as the system is concerned. And yet, as I was beginning to understand, that very system must take some responsibility for the wretchedness of the people without power—for the lack of initiative in their lives, for their dependency upon the handouts of the power people, even for the crimes they commit out of sheer rebellion and desperation.

Granted, there are criminals who will be criminals whatever their situation in life, but they are in the minority. The great majority of the underprivileged are suffering not only from a lack of attention to their needs, both spiritual and practical, but from the system's refusal to acknowledge that they have any needs at all. They have been left alone to deal with the pressures that would drive anyone to destructive acts. When no one else cares, a person stops caring what he does.

It is this same lack of spirituality, this same absence of caring, that makes possible the corruption infecting all levels of the system, from the White House aide down to the prison guard who pulls his car up to the gas pump for a tank of stolen gas. If your heart isn't open to the human vibrations, then what does it matter what you take, or who gets hurt? Success is what counts, and success is the accumulation of power. For what? Power and money in themselves aren't evil, but far too rarely do we see them used for anything good. The system concerns itself only with the possession of power, not its use.

I had been part of the system and I had played the power game, but now I had fallen as far away from it as I possibly could. I had become one of the powerless people, a prison inmate completely dependent upon the mercy of a system whose guards shone lights in my face at night but really couldn't have cared whether I was alive or dead. But I knew I was not what the system said I was: nonhuman and worthless. Christ was redefining me through the men and women who were bringing his love right into the prison itself. These people weren't interested in power. They had achieved something far higher: they cared. They were responding to Christ's demands rather than to those of the system.

My family, for instance, might have abandoned me and won a great deal of sympathy from a public that regarded anyone connected with Watergate as a monster. Yet Gail and the children stood by me even though it meant sharing the penalty I rightly had to pay. My friends ignored the apprehension of those who said "it wasn't the wise thing" to associate with me. I'm sure their loyalty cost them something. The Yokefellows, the Rev. and Mrs. Reid, and the men and women from local churches, unlike most people, accepted the prisoner as a brother—in fact, a wounded brother in need of special care. None of them made any speeches or wore any labels, but each time they wrote a letter and each time they came, their presence was telling me that I was a person, someone worthy of Christ's love and forgiveness. They didn't have to tell anyone they were Christians; in the simple giving of their love and care, they said it all.

I knew then that this was the kind of person I wanted to be someday—I wanted to be able to give to other human beings the kind of love I was receiving from Jesus Christ, and I wanted to give it directly, personally. No more of the easy membership in a club that asked little more of me than my attendance at a good lunch and conversation with the person seated next to me, plus a check for my dues. Perhaps those dues accomplished something good, but that was too little for me to give. "I've allowed you to see the depravity of human nature," God was saying to me, "and for a reason. You can be a voice against this kind of injustice. You can care."

Compared to that, my former goals seemed small. I remembered how proud I had been that I was able to earn a living in the months before I was sentenced. I had survived, which in itself was an achievement. But survival wasn't the most important thing in the world any more. Life was more than that. How would I survive and for what, those were the questions.

As I looked back on my life from inside the prison, everything I had accomplished seemed insignificant compared to being able to care—the moments a perfect stranger reached into his life and gave to me, the smile that erased the tired lines in my wife's face, the shrill laughter of my children who refused to let the prison atmosphere inhibit their play, or the fellow inmate who prayed that Christ would lift the burden of guilt from me. Or the letter written by a friend, Robert Gadberry, who was Nixon's Campaign Chairman in Kansas, in which he said:

> . . . I believe in the basic character and goodness of Jeb Magruder. . . . You have admitted your mistakes and you are continuing to pay a price for it. However, I want you to know I have great admiration and confidence in you. Never let yourself believe bad things about you! Oh, I know how you are filled with regrets and doubt, but this is one of those storms of life that will surely drive roots deeper and make you infallible in conscience and strong in will for the rest of your productive life. . . . Keep faith in God for He is a refuge in times of trial. . . .

Caring means relating your resources to someone else's need—doing whatever you can to help, even if it isn't much at all. It means showing another person that Christ loves him wherever he is, whatever he has done. Even in prison, you can care.

Ever since meeting Doc Benjamin I had worried about him. I wanted to help him, yet I didn't know how. Somehow I always thought he needed something that I didn't have the energy or the training to give. And his was only one of many needs I saw around me.

Doc was Jewish, but he was interested in Christianity and used to ask me questions about my faith. I felt a little awkward about answering his questions because I knew I had much theology to learn before I could discuss the basics of Christianity intelligently. Then I realized that Louie, who certainly could discuss the basics in depth, spoke to me in quite another way when he came to visit me. By his presence, by his concern for my needs at that moment, by the warmth of his conversation, he was talking to me not about the basics, but about Christ himself. He was caring as Christ cared, and that was what was sustaining me spiritually.

I began to talk to Doc about my faith in ordinary terms, telling him as honestly as I could how Jesus Christ had changed my life and my way of looking at things. It felt comfortable—for both of us, I think.

Then one Sunday morning as I was about to go to church I looked at Doc sitting on his bed alone, and I said, "Hey, Doc, do you think you might like to come to church with me?"

He lifted his head and thought a moment. "Sure, why not," he replied, stretching and standing up. He looked at the Bible in my hand. "Should I bring anything?"

"No, Doc, just yourself."

He enjoyed the service, and he came back a

couple of times. It seemed to make a difference in his life.

The more I understood that Christianity is a relationship, the more clearly I could interpret what God was saying to me about the future. He was telling me to take a direction that was entirely different from anything I had known. I had already made it in the world, he was saying, and if I'd been left to my own decisions I probably would go right out and try to make it again. I had been knocked down before, although never quite so hard or down so far, yet, I always got up, more determined than ever to succeed. Now that was all over.

There couldn't be any compromise with the system; it was their way or no way at all. "You can't go back to that kind of life, Jeb," God was saying. "You know what human need is now, and you can't turn your back on it. You have to get involved with people, give them part of yourself, give them what I'm giving you."

In other words, he wanted me to care.

I had no idea how I was going to earn a living outside the system, but somehow that didn't seem to be the most important thing in my life any longer. Nor did I expect that Christ would answer all my questions right away. I had some practical problems to work out—but I had plenty of time to think about them. And maybe that was good.

8

Watch Out for Carl

CARL, THE NEW CLERK in the foreman's office, seemed like the kind of person Bud Krogh had advised me to avoid. Perhaps he wasn't mentally unbalanced in the clinical sense, but he must have been close to it. Prisoners, in general, are paranoid, but this man's symptoms were extreme. He thought everyone was out to get him.

Carl was new to Allenwood. Although he implied that he had Mafia connections, he wasn't accepted by the prison mafioso. In fact, he didn't seem to fit in anywhere except with a small group of troublemakers who looked up to him because he was more educated and articulate than they were. He held a particular grudge against Doc Benjamin who, he claimed, was responsible for his rejection by white-collar prisoners.

As far as I knew, no one was against Carl and Doc barely knew him. But Carl seemed compelled to blame someone for his own hostility, and Doc was as good a choice as any. Ordinarily I would have kept my distance from him, but since we worked together, I couldn't.

I had replaced the head clerk after he was paroled, and I was breaking Carl into my former job. He took a special interest in the Xerox machine in an office in the main building. Usually I did the Xeroxing, but one day Carl asked me if he could do it.

"Sure," I answered.

"You see, I'm trying to get my conviction set aside, and I've got all kinds of correspondence I have to get copied. I thought maybe I could slip a few of my own papers in with the office records. Okay?"

I knew it wasn't a good idea, but I felt sorry for him. There really wasn't any other way he could get copies made. Still, I thought I ought to level with him. "I don't think it's worth the risk you're taking, but if you want to, go ahead. It's your business."

"Thanks, Magruder," he said, taking my folder.

"Watch out for the 'hack' up there," I warned him. "He's no fool."

"I hear he's a hothead," Carl said. "But you don't have any trouble with him, do you?"

"Not so far," I replied.

So from then on Carl did the Xeroxing—until he was caught. Typically, Carl couldn't accept the fact that he had been careless, and he suspected a conspiracy against him.

"How come you never got hassled by the 'hack', Magruder?"

"I never gave him any reason. That's my policy —keep a low profile."

"Or maybe it's because you pass on little bits of information to him, huh?"

I saw what he was getting at. "Look, Carl," I said, "the fact is, you got caught because you did something stupid. That's all there is to it."

"Now I can't even go near that machine, so how am I going to work on my case?" He squinted at me suspiciously. "You'd like that, wouldn't you, Magruder? You and your buddy, that crackpot doctor? You told the guard about me, didn't you?"

"No, and I don't think anyone else did, either."

He shook his head slowly. "I thought you were an okay guy, but it turns out I was wrong. I don't like that kind of stuff, Magruder."

I turned back to my work and tried to ignore him. We never discussed his accusation again, which was just as well, because I couldn't very well prove my innocence to him as long as he was so determined to blame everyone but himself. But every now and then I would look up to see Carl staring at me. Sometimes, in the mess hall, where he ate with the group who now regarded him as their leader, he tried to shake me up by pointing to me and then whispering to the inmates around him.

He was succeeding in worrying me, but there wasn't anything I could do about it.

"He'll get over it," I told Doc Benjamin, who advised me to be careful.

"Not that one," Doc cautioned.

"Magruder, wake up."

I opened my eyes, then closed them quickly in the glare of the guard's flashlight.

"Got two marshals waiting—don't be long," the guard urged.

The night before I had been told that I was to be called to testify at a Watergate-related hearing in Washington the next day, but no one told me what time to be ready to leave Allenwood. I sat up and looked at the illuminated dial of my watch. It was 4 A. M.

When I put on my civilian clothes I saw how much weight I had lost. My suit hung on me. But it felt good to get out of khakis. One of the marshals took out a pair of handcuffs and told me to hold out my hands.

"Sorry," he said, "but it's regulations." I had forgotten about that bit of prison protocol. One of the reasons they were doing it was to show the other prisoners that there wasn't anything special about me. Once we were away from the prison grounds, the handcuffs were removed.

By car the trip to Washington should have taken about four hours, so I was wondering why they awakened me so early in the morning. But we didn't go all the way by car. We drove to the Harrisburg airport, which took about three hours, waited a long time for a plane, and then flew to Washington— why, I'll never know. The trip took seven hours.

In October of 1973 Archibald Cox had been fired by President Nixon in the "Saturday Night Massacre." Cox was replaced by a well-respected Texas attorney, Leon Jaworski, who decided to retain the Cox team of prosecutors rather than delay the Watergate trial by appointing an entirely new staff. Besides, Jaworski knew the trial evidence had already been gathered, and he was more concerned with the difficult task of getting the Nixon tapes. So, as far as I could tell, Jaworski made no difference in the way the prosecutors did their job. Vollner, Ben-Veniste, and the others were still there.

I spent most of that first day in the prosecutors'

offices, sometimes going over old testimony and sometimes just waiting. The hearing had been called by Judge Sirica in response to a claim by Gordon Strachan, one of the Watergate defendants, that his case was tainted and therefore he could not be prosecuted. Gordon's attorneys were arguing that the prosecutors' evidence against him had been obtained directly from him and not from other witnesses. Since the evidence he had given could not be used against him, his attorneys claimed it was "tainted." The prosecutors claimed they had gathered enough evidence against Gordon from others involved in the case. Now it was up to the judge to settle the issue.

I had heard that Herb Kalmbach and Chuck Colson were at Fort Holabird in Baltimore and I assumed I would be sent there, too, but toward the end of the day Jill Vollner told me I would have to spend the night in the Arlington County Jail. Holabird was filled up and would soon be closed, she said. It never occurred to me to question that statement, and I don't know what good it would have done anyway. But since I only had to stay a night or so, one jail seemed as good, or as bad, as another.

I was wrong. I know now that a county jail—new, old or redesigned—is about as bad as a jail can be. It is intended to be a place where men are kept while awaiting trial, and because it is assumed that no one will be there long, no provisions are made for the survival of the human spirit. Being there is the next best thing to being in a zoo.

The Arlington County Jail is on the top floor of the County Courthouse. It was late in July when I was there, and there was no air conditioning in the prisoners' quarters. As we climbed the stairs to the third floor, I could feel that heavy, humid Washington heat growing more intense.

I had been in the company of federal marshals and prosecutors all day, yet I was given a body search. In place of my civilian clothes I was handed pants and a shirt made of stiff, gray material, both much too large for me. Then I was assigned to the "Honor Tank," where, the guard told me, I would probably be safe because I would be in with the best-behaved prisoners.

The "tank" was a cellblock where eight men spent their days and nights, except for the one hour a week when they were taken up on the roof for exercise. Within the cellblock, which was about twenty-four by twelve feet, there were four cells, each about four feet wide by six feet long, with doors removed. In each cell there was a double-tiered iron bed with a dirty mattress, a pillow, and a blanket. Outside these "private" cells was a large open area with a long bench facing the outer bars of the cell block. At one end was an open toilet and a sink; at the other end was a shower, actually nothing more than an open lead pipe. There were no windows. Beyond the outer bars was a television set, a large fan, more cellblocks, and a kitchen which could be smelled rather than seen. The absence of windows and the bluish light coming from long fluorescent bulbs overhead gave the place an unreal, Orwellian appearance.

I had arrived too late for dinner, but I wasn't hungry. The filth of the jail had taken away my appetite. I looked at the seven men sharing the cellblock with me—three of them black and four white—and felt as if someone had opened a door and pushed me into hell itself. The most depressed inmate in Allenwood was alert by comparison. These men didn't move; they didn't lift their heads or focus their eyes. The blank expression on their faces testified to the numbness of their senses, and perhaps their minds.

A little later I tried talking to some of them, but conversation was all but impossible.

"How long have you been here?" I'd ask.

"Six months, about," was a typical answer, although in some cases it was longer.

"Well, what about your trial? When is it scheduled for?"

"Don't know. Just never seems to get here."

"Six months—what do you do all day?"

"Nothin'."

There was nothing these men *could* do except walk from one part of the cellblock to another. Imagine yourself living in the largest room in your home along with seven other human beings and never getting out, except for one hour a week. Then imagine yourself doing it for months, with no end in sight. The only way to remain sane would be to withdraw, which is what these men did. But they had withdrawn so far and for such a long time that I wondered whether they would ever be able to lead a reasonably normal life again. Sharing that small space with me, they were the most remote men I have ever seen.

The intended purpose of the county jail is a farce, since many of the inmates spend as long as eighteen months there, either awaiting trial or, having been convicted, awaiting assignment to a prison. Almost without exception, the men I saw were uneducated about their rights and could not afford legal representation. So they were represented by public defenders who usually mean well but can't spend much time with each client.

The visiting regulations were the worst imaginable. A wood partition separated the visitor from the prisoner, so they couldn't even see each other. They communicated through a microphone installed in the partition.

The bed was uncomfortable and too short, but that wasn't the only reason I couldn't sleep that night. The television set was on until two in the morning and those cold fluorescent lights never went out. The noise level was high—a nervous blend of radios, arguments, weeping and moaning, and bodies tossing restlessly on iron bunks in the oppressive nighttime heat. I lay on my back, almost guiltily aware that I would be leaving the next morning and at the very worst would be spending only one other night there. How must it feel to wonder if you would ever get out? And didn't anyone care?

The next morning a guard brought me my civilian clothes and a razor so I could shave. I tried to take a shower under the open pipe, steeling myself for the cold water that fell rather than poured out, but I had to give up the effort. Breakfast was a disaster. The eggs, the coffee, everything, was cold. I couldn't eat.

Out in the hallway, where the guard had taken me to meet the marshals, a medic passed me and stopped. "You don't look so well," he observed.

"I don't feel so well," I answered.

He left and then returned with some Valium capsules. "Take these—you need them," he said, handing me a paper cup full of water with one hand and the capsules in the other.

The Valium was intended to calm me, which it did, but it also relaxed my self-control, and by the time the marshals appeared I was in tears. I was able to pull myself together for a little while, but soon after we arrived at the prosecutors' offices I came apart again. It happened while I was talking on the phone to Gail, telling her that she had better not plan to visit me in the Arlington County Jail. If I had been affected by the misery I had seen, Gail would have been devastated. As I was talking, I choked up and burst into tears.

Jill Vollner happened to walk into the room at that moment and for the first time I saw her expression soften into something like compassion. She and the marshals were kind and sympathetic as they waited for me to recover, but for the longest time they completely misunderstood what had happened. Finally I was able to explain to them that I was going to be all right, but the men in the county jail weren't.

"Have you ever been there?" I asked Jill.

"No," she replied, "and I apologize for sending you there."

"That's not the point," I went on. "You're in the business of sending people to jail. Don't you think you ought to find out what a jail is like? I know you won't believe what I'm telling you—but go and see for yourself!"

"I will," she promised, almost too eagerly. And then I realized what really was getting to her as she turned to one of the marshals and said, "He'll never be fit to testify if we don't snap him out of this." The wasting men in the county jail didn't concern her; it was my performance on the witness stand that did.

I remembered some conversations I'd had with Jill in between interrogating sessions the previous summer. I used to ask her questions about her basic philosophy of life, assuming that she probably had some pretty strong feelings about her work. She did, but they weren't related to justice, truth, or mercy. She was much more interested in the publicity she hoped to get from being in on the Watergate trial and thought it would lead to an important job in the power structure of government. It sounded all too familiar, and as I recalled those talks, I knew it wasn't likely she would ever take a ride over to the Arlington County Jail. She was going through the motions of compassion, and once I got myself together that would be the end of it. Jill even sent for a Justice Department investigator who spent some time asking me questions about the conditions in the jail, but as far as I know, no one of any authority ever set foot there to confirm that report—if there ever really was a report. But recently I read that Jill Vollner was appointed Legal Counsel for the Department of the Army.

That afternoon several of us testified at the hearing. (Later, much to the annoyance of the prosecutors, Gordon Strachan won his point and his case was declared tainted.) When the session ended, everyone was asked to rise, but Judge Sirica, instead of leaving the courtroom first, as judges customarily do, came down from the bench and walked over to me.

"How are you, Jeb?" he asked.

"Okay, your honor," I answered.

"How's your family?" he continued.

"They're doing well, your honor."

The judge shook his head slightly. "I know this must be tough on them—and on you," he said. "I just hope you're all getting along as well as can be expected under the circumstances. I know it isn't easy." Then he said good-by and left the courtroom.

Most of us can tell when someone means what he says, and there was no mistaking the sincerity of this man who was so aware that beneath all the precedents, briefs, and principles, justice dealt with human lives. For him, compassion was not pretense.

That night I didn't go back to the county jail. All of a sudden the prosecutors "discovered" that Holabird was not filled up or closing, and they sent me there. Of course, it hadn't been filled the night before either. The next day I was taken back to Allenwood, which looked rather good to me.

That afternoon I told Johnny Sample about the jail. "Hell on earth, " he muttered.

"You've been there?" I said.

"Not Arlington. I was in the Philadelphia House of Detention, which has the honor of being almost the worst in the country."

"How long were you there?"

"Ten months, man." Johnny didn't want to talk about it. He stood up and changed the subject.

"How about a game?" he suggested, reaching for his tennis racket.

Toward the end of August my lawyers told me I would be transferred to Fort Holabird indefinitely. After several delays and legal maneuverings by the many defense attorneys involved, the Watergate trial was finally scheduled to begin in October and the prosecutors wanted their witnesses close by. I looked forward to the change of address, particularly because it meant Gail and the children wouldn't have to drive so far to visit me.

The day I received the news, the warden told me to be ready to leave the next morning. I knew I would be returning to Allenwood after I testified, so I put most of my books and my radio in my cabinet, which now had a combination lock. I kept out a few books and my Bible to take to Holabird.

I was getting some letters together when Doc Benjamin came over to my bunk and stood over me. "Jeb, I was just over in Bill Edwards' dorm," he said, "and I think you ought to know what I overheard." He looked shaken.

"You know that guy who works with you? Carl?" he asked.

I nodded.

"Well, I was on my way out, passing by his bunk, when I heard him say to a couple of men, 'Tonight's the night we get Magruder.' "

At first I thought Carl must have heard I was leaving. But then I thought, *No, he probably doesn't know—and that just might help me.* No one knew I was leaving, not even Doc Benjamin, and I decided to keep it that way.

"Thanks, Doc," I said.

"Jeb, I hope you take me seriously," Doc went on.

"I do, Doc. And I know Carl—he's like that."

"Don't you think you ought to tell the guard?" Doc continued.

"You really think he'll believe me?" I replied.

Doc shook his head and sat down on my bunk. "No, not a chance. I should have known better. Jeb, what'll you do?"

I closed the cabinet door and turned the lock, "I don't know, Doc—but I'm sure not going to sleep."

I made it my business to stay in the brightly-lit lobby all night watching television and talking to anyone who was there. Since I didn't see Carl or any of the men I recognized as his friends, I was hoping the threat was only tough talk—the kind you can expect in prison. But, knowing Carl's suspicion of me, I wasn't taking any chances.

Though I was uneasy, I was not afraid—I hadn't lost the feeling that God was with me and that he would help me deal with the prison experience, so in a sense I already felt protected. But I wasn't invulnerable. I prayed, "Lord, protect me."

This time, when the two marshals came for me at four in the morning, I was wide awake and ready to leave. And I was glad the warden hadn't given me time to tell anyone I was going.

9

Fort Holabird

THE WAY I LOOK AT IT, I was doing society a
favor," Skitch said as we jogged side by side around
the one-mile track. It had been a road in Fort Holabird's heyday during World War II. "I mean, the
only guys I killed were criminals—except for three
cops, and that was an accident."

Skitch had been a Mafia hit man. He had killed
twenty-seven men and never got caught. But then he
grew careless. In between Mafia assignments, he
tried robbing banks, and in one robbery three po-
licemen were killed. Skitch was caught and probably would have gone to prison for life, except that he
was able to make a deal. In exchange for a sentence
reduced to ten years, he confessed to his backlog of

murders and gave evidence against the mob who hired him.

Skitch was a big man who liked to keep in shape, which is how we got to know each other quite well. I was running five miles a day by then, and Skitch had been running at least that much before I arrived. He also used the weights in the exercise room.

If anyone had told me back in Washington that my career would include running alongside a hired killer, I would have called him crazy. And sometimes, even while it was happening, I found it hard to believe. I don't know what I expected a hit man to be like. Probably, in common with most people whose only association with the mob is the TV screen, I thought a killer was some kind of a monster, anything but human. Well, I had a lot to learn.

In fact, Skitch was a very nice guy and I liked him. He had a wife he cared a lot about and a young son whose violent nature was going to land him in trouble, but he didn't seem to know what to do about either one of them. Skitch had enough problems of his own, and staying alive must have been at the top of his list. Naturally the mob wanted him dead, and in almost any prison they could have arranged to have him killed.

But Holabird was not "any" prison. It was a "safe house," which means exactly what it says—a place where certain prisoners can be kept safe, or, more specifically, alive. Such security measures were evidently necessary for the Watergate witnesses. Holabird was also convenient to Washington where the Watergate trial would take place, and there was room for us, at least for a while. For the other prisoners, the safe house was even more important because it offered the kind of protection they could not get in an ordinary prison. They were men who had given testimony against their former friends and associates in crime, and for them no amount of security was too much. Even when Skitch and I ran, two marshals in a car followed us, always ready to scoop us up at the slightest indication of trouble.

During World War II, Fort Holabird must have been impressive. It had been the headquarters for the Army Security Agency, which meant it was more than an ordinary military base. Many officers and their families used to live there in two-story brick houses surrounded by shrubs and rosebushes. The roses were in full bloom and the grass was neatly clipped, but the houses were empty now. Only two buildings were still in use—one by the ASA, which still did some translating work and employed a number of local people, and one by federal marshals and the prisoners they guarded. Going through the gates made a person feel a little like Goldilocks entering the home of the three bears and seeing all that porridge with no one around to eat it.

Compared to Allenwood, Holabird offered an immediate advantage—privacy. There were only eighteen and, sometimes, twenty inmates. Each of us had his own room plus a bath shared with another inmate. Our building had been a bachelor officers' dormitory, which is why there were so many rooms. It was wonderful to feel four walls around me and have a door I could close.

Because Holabird was being phased out, we presented a unique problem to the prison system. Bureaucracy that it was, it couldn't cope with such a small and impermanent unit. Consequently, some of the usual regulations weren't enforced—not because they couldn't have been, but because no one seemed to know how to adapt the rules to a small, temporary group. For instance, the authorities decided that prison uniforms were out because there was no prison laundry to keep them clean. Instead, we inmates were allowed to wear our own civilian clothing, which we laundered in washers and dryers installed for our use. The same was true of a kitchen. The prison authorities thought it was a waste of time to set up a standard kitchen and designate inmate cooks, so they allowed each of us to prepare our own food in the bachelor officers' kitchen. Each inmate received eight dollars a day to cover the cost of his food, which at that time was quite generous.

The guards were armed federal marshals, and there were eight of them. This was a sizable group for such a small number of prisoners, but at least it kept the inmates from worrying about trouble from other inmates or people on the outside. Every two weeks the marshals were transferred, so we never came to know any of them well.

The inmates were different from the street criminals I had known at Allenwood. One was Paul Noe, a con man of such exceptional skill that the FBI frequently "borrowed" him to conduct seminars for its agents in the finer points of con games. Another was Bill Turnblazer, president of the local mineworkers' union through which the payoff money in the Yablonski murders was funneled. Turnblazer himself turned the money over to Tony Boyle, and was doing ten years for it. He told me that at the time he didn't know how the money was going to be used. Both were pleasant, interesting men, and talking to them helped me pass the time.

Most of the others were Mafia men or Mafia-related. A few were fairly high up in the mob hierarchy. Several others claimed to be, but actually weren't; they were hit men and muscle men—like Skitch—hired or used by the mob, but not necessarily part of it.

Some of the others were men involved in international drug traffic, citizens of Mexico and Central American countries. They all claimed that their local authorities and the FBI had tricked or forced them onto planes which delivered them to the United States, where they were immediately arrested. Information was the price they were paying for a reduction of charges against them.

Then there were the Watergate trial witnesses: Herb Kalmbach, John Dean, Charles Colson, and I.

Herb Kalmbach had been transferred from a California prison. His family still lived out there and he missed them. Though his wife wanted to come east to be near him, Herb didn't want to subject her to the Holabird environment. I understood how he felt, and I sometimes doubted the wisdom of allowing Gail and the children to visit me. The sight of marshals with guns tucked into their belts was frightening. Then there were the other inmates. Their language was unbelievably profane even for adult ears, and the presence of young children—sometimes their own—didn't seem to inhibit them.

I liked Herb. He was a quiet, considerate man who was taking prison hard—with good reason. One of Herb's dreams as a young man had been to form one of the most prestigious, successful law firms in the Los Angeles area, and he had made that dream come true. His firm was among the best known and most respected. But now all that was gone. Herb had been disbarred and could never practice law again. He left the firm in disgrace. Fortunately he has just been reinstated by the California Bar Association.

Chuck Colson had been at Holabird but was transferred to another prison in Alabama. He would be back before the trial.

So far John Dean had not been imprisoned at all, but right after Labor Day he came to Holabird to begin serving his sentence. It was typical of Dean that he did things a little differently than anyone else, and that included the way he spent his time in jail. He came accompanied by a federal marshal who kept guard outside his door, which was a greater security measure than that taken for inmates who had testified against the mob. For that reason, Herb and I didn't see much of him at first, which didn't really bother us because, frankly, we weren't exactly eager to see him. We just didn't know what to expect when John Dean was present, because we knew his computerlike mind was always clicking, always figuring an angle. Talking to him was a definite risk because he had a way of distorting the conversation at a later date so that he would come out on top, with everyone else on the bottom.

We never knew what kind of a deal Dean had made with the prosecutors, but his arrangement obviously was different from ours. Although he hadn't been successful in getting immunity, he seemed to have many privileges to make life more comfortable for him. He spent little time at Holabird because almost every day he went to the prosecutors' offices. In the morning a car and driver arrived to pick him up, and off he went, dressed in a business suit and sitting in the back seat, reading the newspaper. He never came back until evening. Except for weekends, he spent only the nights in prison.

I didn't think the prosecutors could possibly be working with Dean that much. They had me coming in about twice a week for a few weeks before the trial, and even though Dean had more information to review, I didn't see how it could take five full days every week for such a long time. Then a friend of mine who worked for the prosecutors told me that Dean wasn't just going over his trial testimony. A good part of the time he was sitting in an office by himself, using the telephone. To a prisoner, unlimited access to a telephone was the ultimate luxury.

I found the prosecutors even more difficult to deal with now that I was a prisoner. They seemed eager to impress me with the fact that I was not free to come and go. Since I was always in the company of a marshal, I hardly needed to be reminded of that fact.

As a trial witness I had the right to consult an attorney, so frequently it was necessary to call one of my lawyers and ask his advice about something that came up in my conversations with the prosecutors. Usually it was a simple matter of asking to use the phone and dialing the number. But one day at lunchtime I needed to talk to Jim Sharp. I asked one of the men on the prosecutors' staff where I could use a telephone.

He pointed to Jill Vollner's office. "Use the one in there," he said. And I did.

I was talking to Jim when Jill returned from lunch. She opened the door and when she saw me she went into a rage. "What are you doing in here!" she screamed at me. "You have no right to be in here! Put that phone down and get out!"

I asked Jim to hold on. "Don't get upset, Jill," I said, trying to calm her down. "I'm talking to my lawyer—and I do have that right."

"What are you doing in my office?" she shouted.

"I asked where I could use a phone, and someone told me to use yours," I replied.

The marshal, who had been standing just outside the door, was looking from Jill to me in confusion. I think he was trying to figure out what I had done wrong. Finally the reality of the situation began getting through to Jill and she regained control of herself. "I'm sorry," she apologized. "You just took me by surprise. I'd rather you didn't use my phone."

Fortunately, I didn't always have such a hard time getting to a phone, and occasionally I was able to call Gail while I was in Washington. That was a real privilege for me because, back at Holabird, there was only one phone and someone was always using it.

A week after I arrived at Holabird I was due for my first weekend furlough. This was a special privilege granted to minimum-security prisoners after they had been in prison a certain length of time, and while I was still in Allenwood my application for furlough had been approved. Neither the prosecutors nor the marshals expressed any concern about my spending Labor Day weekend away, so I didn't see any reason why I shouldn't begin to look forward to it. Gail, the children and I were planning to spend that time at a friend's farm in Pennsylvania— away from prison, home, and everyone who knew us. We just wanted to be together.

The night before Gail was supposed to pick me up, I was called to the office of the marshal in charge of the safe house. He was a moody older man we used to call "Colonel Klink," after one of the characters in the TV series, "Hogan's Heroes." Brusquely he told me there would be no furlough. There was too much red tape involved because of my transfer to Holabird, and neither prison would accept responsibility for me during a furlough. When Colonel Klink saw the look on my face, he said I shouldn't be so upset about missing a couple of days with my wife and children. How would he know? He wasn't married. He had no family.

I could picture Gail and the kids loading the car with our tennis shoes and rackets and some basketballs, and all kinds of good things to eat. I dreaded calling home and instead I called my lawyers to see if they could do anything to help. They tried to persuade the Bureau of Prisons to change the ruling regarding responsibility for transfers, but were unsuccessful.

Finally I had to call Gail. She tried not to cry, and I fought the lump rising in my throat as I heard the kids asking questions in the background. I didn't want to think about them unloading the car, but I couldn't avoid it. I felt so helpless to do anything to ease their disappointment.

Not long after I left Holabird, Colonel Klink was dismissed. He had gone to the apartment of a prisoner's wife and tried to assault her, threatening her with reprisals to her husband if she resisted him. But she did resist, and had the courage to report him to his superiors.

Some of the marshals were very considerate. A few times one of them took me to the Ellipse at lunchtime where we met Gail and had a picnic lunch. And I'll never forget the man who made it possible for me to see my son on his birthday.

It was the end of a long day and time to go back to Holabird. Tired from a particularly difficult session with the prosecutors, I slumped down in the front seat next to the marshal.

"Well, your boy's got a nice day for his birthday," the marshal commented.

For a moment I wondered how he knew it was Stuart's birthday, but then I remembered that I had mentioned it that morning. Gail had invited some of Stuart's friends to the house for a small party, and I was hoping the weather would be good.

"Yeah," I answered and got ready to fall asleep.

A few minutes later I sat up, wide awake. I was so accustomed to the ride back to Holabird that I knew every turn, and even in my half-sleep I realized we were going the wrong way. We were headed toward my house.

I looked at the marshal and he shook his head. "Let's keep this to ourselves, okay?" he said. "I could lose my job if it got around."

I couldn't have said a word, anyway. Suddenly I choked up. It didn't seem real being on our street again, then slowing down to turn into the driveway. The garage door was open, as usual, and the marshal pulled in right next to Gail's car. I waited while he got out and closed the garage door.

Someone had heard us. The door to the house opened and there was Gail, staring and not believing what she saw. The children pushed past her and ran to the car, pulling the door open and heaving themselves in on top of me.

"Happy birthday, Stu," I said as his arms tightened around my neck.

His voice was shrill with excitement. "Daddy! Daddy!" he shouted. "You came to my party!" He didn't care how I got there.

The party was over by then and the guests had gone home, so we had another party all by ourselves. It was a short one because the marshal and I couldn't stay long. But the visit was enough to make a little boy very happy. Not to mention his father.

Chuck Colson was transferred back to Holabird in September, just before the trial began. I suppose most people assumed that we four Watergate men would be pretty close in prison, but things didn't work out that way. We split down the middle. Chuck Colson and John Dean seemed obsessed with what they called "the Case," and they kept going over and over the whole Watergate sequence of events, almost as if they thought they might find something that would tell them it had never happened. Herb Kalmbach and I spent a lot of time together, but Watergate was the last thing we wanted to talk about. We had been there. We knew it was real, and we wanted to get beyond it.

Once, when Doug Coe came to see Chuck, he was upset because Chuck had made no effort to share his Christian experience with me.

"It's okay," I said. "I think I understand how Chuck feels. We had a lot of disagreements in the past, so maybe we need more time as Christians."

I've noticed that many people expect all Christians to like each other on sight, or at least to get along together simply because they are Christians. But you can't omit the human factor. Some people are mutually antagonistic to each other, and being Christians doesn't change that. The history of Christianity is filled with conflicting opinions—and even the apostles had their disagreements. What does make a difference is that Christians can work at reducing the antagonisms. If they can't love each other as they are, then they have to let the Christ in each of them do the loving through them—and that takes time. I think that's where Chuck and I were then: we were working at reducing the antagonisms between us, and in some ways we still are. One of these days we'll get there.

A few days after Doug Coe's visit, Chuck suggested that the four of us get together and read the Bible. That was a good start and it meant something to all of us. We did it several times.

Chuck's path and mine often cross now that we are out of prison. He is an indefatigable Christian, performing a genuine ministry to men who are still behind bars. He is also sensitive to human distress even when it is unuttered—I know that from personal experience.

He called us recently. It was shortly after the TV series, "Washington: Behind Closed Doors," ended, and Gail and I were feeling pretty bruised. The series was based on a novel by John Ehrlichman, who chose to tell the Watergate story in fictionalized form. The result was sort of a tease for most viewers —the events and characters were changed just enough to call it "fiction" (and possibly to protect the author from libel suits), but anyone who had kept up with Watergate could guess who the characters were supposed to be. Well, the Jeb Magruder character

was bad enough—but the distortion of Gail was brutal. I think that's why Chuck called. He also had
been worked over by the script and he knew how we
felt. He and I had been through that sort of thing before, and, although it still hurt, we knew that some
people just never were going to forgive us for our part
in Watergate. But the attack on Gail, an innocent
victim, was deliberate and cruel, and Chuck sensed
her pain.

"I just want you to know that Patty and I are
sorry you had to suffer all over again," he said.
"And Gail—the people who know you and love you
know that what they saw on the screen wasn't true."

Gail and I appreciated that.

The best thing about Holabird was knowing Gail
didn't have to drive so far to visit me. And it was
good to have a room where we and the children
could be together as a family. A few times the marshals allowed us to go out in a field beyond the fence
and play touch football, which kept the children
from getting restless during their visits.

I stopped worrying about the effect of the inmates' language on my children. Most of the time
the children didn't seem to notice anything except
that the men used some pretty "funny" words.

As a family we were much more closely involved
in the lives of the other inmates than we had been at
Allenwood because we weren't confined to a crowded
visiting area. For a while we inmates and our visitors
used to eat together on visiting days until the warden
decided to discontinue that privilege. But we often
shared a pot of coffee in the kitchen or talked together in the TV room, and sometimes we visited
with other inmates and their families in their rooms.

I'm sure the Watergate men seemed as alien to
the other inmates as they seemed to us at first. In
fact, the Watergate breakin was such a petty crime,

in their eyes, that they wondered why we were in prison at all, unless it was for tripping over our own feet. The political implications and the immorality of what we had done meant nothing to them because they couldn't identify with those aspects of life. The only politics they knew were the unvarying rules by which the mob lived: you broke a rule and you were killed; you destroyed the opposition before it destroyed you; the more you were feared, the stronger you became. Morality had no place in their environment because crime was not a separate and illegal act—it was a way of life. As Skitch said, he felt he was giving society a fringe benefit because the men he killed were criminals.

Eventually these men would go back into society with new identities put together by the federal government in an effort to protect them from retaliation. But in most cases the new identities weren't going to fit because the men would be the same. They didn't know any other way to make a living. With no friends beside those whom they had betrayed, they would sooner or later drift back to the old haunts, and someone would recognize them. And that would be the end of it.

They knew it and didn't try to fool themselves about it. Expecting to be killed, they were trying to hold on to life as long as they could.

I thought Skitch might make it because at least he was trying to change his way of life as well as his name. "I'm going to take a course in air conditioning repairs," he informed me one day.

"Isn't that kind of seasonal work?" I asked.

"Not compared to robbing a bank, it isn't," he replied, and we both laughed.

Skitch was practically living on tranquilizers when I first met him, but I think all the running we did was beginning to clear up his head. At first he would nod all the time and hardly say a word, but now we were able to have a decent conversation. Holabird would be closed down soon, he knew, and that meant he would be sent to another prison. He was hoping it wouldn't be one clear across the country where his wife wouldn't be able to visit him. It worried him to have her on her own.

"Couldn't she move out to wherever you have to go?" I asked. Money never seemed to be a problem with Skitch—or any of the other inmates, for that matter—so I assumed his wife could afford to follow him wherever he went.

"Depends," Skitch replied. "She doesn't like to go too far from her people—and they live around here." He shook his head. "She doesn't make friends too easy."

Once I got past the rough language and the awesome criminal records of these men, they were like the rest of us—scared and wondering what to do with the rest of their lives. But they were cut off from anyone who could help them, and, worse than that, they had never known any spiritual nourishment.

What could I do for someone like that? I began to wonder whether I should try to tell these men what was happening to me. In spite of the oppressive atmosphere of prison, a new life was growing inside me, and it didn't seem right for me to keep it to myself. I don't know how many times I made up my mind to tell Skitch about Jesus Christ and the way he kept me from feeling I was completely alone— yet I couldn't get started. The words just wouldn't come into my mind, and I felt awkward.

Once when Louie came to see me, I asked him about it. "Maybe you aren't ready to witness yet, Jeb," Louie pointed out. "You know, you have the rest of your life to do that."

He surprised me. "But I'm not going to spend the rest of my life here—at least, I hope not—and where else am I going to run into a need like this?"

"I can't say, and neither can you," he replied. "Only God can do that. He'll pick the time and the place, Jeb, and you'll know it. You won't have to think about the words. Christ will do that for you. He'll simply put them there in your mouth."

I guess I couldn't hide my disappointment. I think I wanted Louie to fire me up and send me in to talk to Skitch with the kind of words that would turn him into an instant Christian.

Louie smiled and shifted to the edge of his chair. "Hey, Jeb—don't get me wrong. I know how you feel. I know you want to give everyone what Christ has given you—and I'm glad. That's beautiful! But you're so young as a Christian. You have so much to learn about how to live as a Christian. Suppose you do start to tell everyone you meet how wonderful it is to have Jesus Christ in your heart? People are going to ask you some pretty tough questions. They'll want to know why? How? Why didn't it happen before? What difference will it make now? Who is Christ? How do you know he's real? And lots more, Jeb. And you won't be doing Christ any favor by not being able to give intelligent, logical, well–informed answers to those questions."

Actually Louie was reminding me of the way I felt before I accepted Christ. At that time, if someone had told me (even in the most sincere words) how much Christ meant to him, I might have backed away. I would probably have been reluctant to allow myself to be swept up by so much emotion. It's possible that when the emotions wore off, my mind would have raised too many unanswered questions, and I would have felt let down. Looking back, I had to admire the restraint of the men and women who were such a comfort to me in those days. They must have felt much as I did now, seeing a person so in need of Christ and wanting to tell him, "Look, here he is!"—but sensing that the time wasn't right. The most important introduction in a person's life is one you don't want to blow—if you can possibly help it.

"There's a lot of pressure on you now, Jeb," Louie told me, "and there'll be a lot more. People want to hear from a converted sinner, especially a famous one, and I'm sure your testimony will do some good—when you're ready to give it."

"But not now," I said, and he nodded agreement. "You're absolutely right, Louie. I'm not ready, and I'm glad you made me aware of that."

"Don't let anyone rush you," he warned. "The more you wait, the more you'll have to say."

Already I was feeling greatly relieved. For a while I had felt awkward talking to Skitch and some of the other men because I kept thinking I should be giving them something of spiritual significance. After all, I was a Christian. But the Christians who had helped me never tried to evangelize me in so many words; they simply loved me as Christ loved me, and that was the best thing I could do for the men in prison with me. Later it would be time for words, and maybe someone else would speak them. Christ had other work for me to do now.

The worst thing about Holabird was the boredom. There was absolutely nothing to do from the time we woke up until we went to sleep, and at times I found myself wishing I were back in Allenwood with my clerical job. At least it made the time pass more quickly.

I read a lot, but you can't read all day and all evening. Just to keep busy, I painted my room three times. We took turns doing the cooking, so each man had kitchen duty only once in eighteen days.

All of us looked forward to the few times we were able to leave Holabird. I can't say I enjoyed going to the prosecutors' offices, but it *was* a change of routine. Once or twice a week some of the Mafia men went out, in the company of marshals, to buy our food. Occasionally the marshals took a few of us out to a movie. I even found myself looking forward to my occasional visits to the U. S. Public Health Service office for my allergy shots.

Fortunately we had the right to attend religious services, and since there were none available in the safe house, we were permitted to attend churches in the Baltimore area—in the company of marshals, of course. I went to First Presbyterian Church in Baltimore where Robert Hewitt, a friend of Louie Evans, was pastor. There again I was accepted with love and support. Once Gail was able to arrive early on Sunday and go to services with me, and once the Hewitts had her stay at their home for the weekend.

Gradually I was gaining some perspective. I was beginning to realize that even though a person has many different responsibilities in life, not all of them are important. In fact, only a few really matter at all: God, my family, and whatever work Christ wanted me to do for him. The prosecutors didn't matter, the trial didn't matter, money didn't matter, and neither did getting ahead. I couldn't avoid all those things, and I had to give some serious thought to making a living after prison, but I couldn't allow them to run my life—to rob me of the time I wanted to spend with God and my family.

So, that meant it was going to be me against the system—probably for the rest of my life.

10

The Watergate Trial

ON SEPTEMBER 8, 1974, when President Gerald
Ford pardoned Richard Nixon, it caused a flurry of
expectancy among the Watergate witnesses at
Holabird. Chuck Colson was sure the President
would also pardon us; the rest of us were not quite
as certain. I don't think I really believed it would
happen, but I couldn't stop myself from hoping. I
wanted to get out as much as anyone.

As far as the pardon itself was concerned, I
wasn't opposed to it. Ever since reading the transcripts of the White House tapes, I was convinced
that the former President had been involved in the
cover-up, and I felt he should be held accountable
for what he had done. In favor of the impeachment

process, I thought the resignation was a sensible response to the evidence accumulated through it. It
spared the nation and the former President the
agony of a long and bitter trial, and both had already suffered enough. For a man like Nixon, resignation was severe punishment. I did not want to see
Richard Nixon in jail. I was there, and I knew that
imprisonment did not accomplish anything except
to protect society from its more dangerous members
(I didn't include Nixon in that category).

But I did feel that the pardon was granted care-
lessly. Wrongs had been committed, and the nation
had a right to a record of those wrongs. I think the
pardon should have been given only in exchange for
a Bill of Particulars detailing Richard Nixon's involvement in the conspiracy—not for publication or
exposure of a man already painfully revealed as less
than honest, but because the nation had a right to
know what his involvement was. Someday Richard
Nixon and his apologists will try to rewrite history,
claiming that this tragic President was betrayed by
his underlings and railroaded out of the office by his
enemies. When that time comes, memories will be
blurred by emotions past and present, and it would
help to have the record at hand. But that wasn't the
way it worked out.

Certainly the timing of the pardon could have
been better. Coming just before the Watergate trial,
it couldn't help but influence the nation's attitude
toward the defendants in that trial. With Nixon forever beyond the reach of the law for any illegal acts
committed during his administration, the public had
to vent its frustrations on the only targets left: Haldeman, Mitchell, Ehrlichmann, Parkinson, and
Mardian. On the other hand, many people would
think it was unfair for those men to suffer punishment while Nixon got off scot free. Either way, it

would be almost impossible for anyone to be objective about the trial.

Within a short time, it was obvious that there would be no pardons for us. Whether or not President Ford intended to get around to us, we didn't know, but the public outcry against the Nixon pardon was too great.

Maybe Sirica will let us go after the trial, we thought. It was possible.

The trial began in mid-October. I was on the stand for five days in November; Dean was on for nine. I had wondered how I would feel giving testimony against men I had worked with so closely only a few years before. But any trace of sentiment was gone. Though I wasn't hoping they would somehow get off, I certainly wasn't rooting for the prosecutors to win. I simply wanted to see justice done.

I felt sorry for John Mitchell. He will always seem like a father to me, although the public had a much different image of him—one he created himself. He liked to play the tough guy to the press, and he hadn't changed. He was still puffing on his pipe and giving short answers, or none at all. The last thing in the world he wanted anyone to know was that he was a compassionate human being underneath it all. Well, I thought, if that's the way he wants it. . . .

Haldeman was something else. He had let his hair grow out of the familiar crew cut that suited his abrasive personality. Now he was playing Mr. Nice Guy who couldn't remember anything that had happened before, during, and after Watergate. In fact, he kept telling the press, he didn't understand how such a terrible thing could have happened. Watching him on TV, answering reporters' questions patiently and in a pleasant tone of voice, even I found it hard to remember that the atmosphere which made Watergate possible was created by Richard Nixon and fortified by H. R. Haldeman. Haldeman's hypocrisy killed whatever respect I had left for him. The events have finally touched Haldeman, too. After Richard Nixon was interviewed by David Frost on television, Haldeman stated that in his forthcoming book he would tell the truth about Watergate, and would directly implicate the President in the case. I have read his book and found it full of self-serving statements rather than the truth. Haldeman apparently neglected to check memos in his files to which I referred in my first book, *An American Life*.

I had no evidence to give against John Ehrlichman, but I had quite a bit relating to Kenneth Parkinson. His lawyer was the only one who really went after me when I was on the stand. His argument was that Parkinson had every reason to think I was lying when I told him the truth about Watergate, because I had told the cover-up lies to so many other people by that time. It was a foolish point to try to make, but that was the way he attempted to destroy my credibility as a witness. The only thing it accomplished was to make me angry enough to fight back, which made the rest of my testimony easier.

Robert Mardian had never been a problem. He and I didn't get along, and that situation hadn't changed. He was coarse and vengeful, but then he had always been that way, so at least he wasn't trying to fool anyone.

Then, suddenly, it ended. All the months of going over and over my testimony were finished by early November. Just before Christmas the trial ended and the jury retired. The letdown was something I hadn't anticipated.

Now I really was left with nothing to do, and worst of all, no place to go. I felt myself slipping down into a depression worse than any I had felt before, and there seemed to be no way I could stop it.

The closer Christmas came, the more we allowed ourselves to think Judge Sirica might let us out in time for the holidays. He had that power. And we had demonstrated our cooperativeness during the trial. But Christmas came and went, and there was no word.

Maybe he'll do it for New Year's, we thought.

I didn't tell Gail or the children about our hopes. If nothing happened, the disappointment would have been too cruel.

Shortly after Christmas the verdicts came in and I noted them without emotion: Haldeman, guilty; Ehrlichman, guilty; Mitchell, guilty; Mardian, guilty; Parkinson, not guilty. Parkinson was the only surprise.

Holabird was going to close down in a few weeks, and I would be sent back to Allenwood. I didn't mind, but I *had* to have something to do. The fact that I might be in danger, because Carl was still there, didn't matter. Inactivity was driving me out of my mind. At least, in Allenwood I would have a job of some sort.

In desperation I began going to a prison psychiatrist because I was afraid that if I slipped any deeper into depression, I wouldn't be able to climb back out. And that helped. The depression didn't go away, but at least I was able to understand what it was and why it happened to me.

Now, when people say to me, "You didn't have it so bad—you were in a minimum-security prison," I make them an offer. "Tell you what," I say. "Why don't you try living in a hotel room—no, make it a suite, and in the best hotel you know. Try living there for six months. Give yourself a TV set, newspapers, books, visits from your friends and family, all the room service you want—and see if you don't get depressed after six months' confinement."

That's what was happening to me. Psychologist Karl Menninger points out that six months is about all the time a person can be confined without becoming severely depressed. The prison psychiatrist agreed with him. And I had been in prison a little over six months by that time. Understanding didn't provide a cure, but it did take much of the fear away. I knew I wasn't going to go insane, but I realized I had to fight this thing that was eating away at my energy and my outlook. That's why I decided to ask to be transferred back to Allenwood as soon as possible. I didn't want to wait for Holabird to close down.

New Year's Day came and, again, there was no word of release, but this time I took the news differently. At the most, I had a little over a year more to serve before satisfying the Parole Board guidelines. For some reason, that didn't seem so bad. God had given me an opportunity to have my family with me at Holabird during the holidays, which was a blessing for all of us, and I was grateful. God was taking care of us, and I could trust him with our future. If he wanted me to remain in prison a while, then that was all right with me. He knew best.

One night about a week after New Year's Day, I was watching the six o'clock news and saw an interview with the head of the Parole Board. The reporter asked him whether the Watergate men stood a good chance of being paroled when they became eligible. His answer was chilling: These were special cases, he said calmly, and the usual parole board guidelines would not apply to them. The board would have to give them special attention because their crimes were so unusual.

Chuck Colson's eyes met mine. We both knew what those words "special attention" meant. Forget about parole—we were going to max out, if this man had anything to say about it. And he certainly did.

I thought of calling my lawyer to tell him about the interview, but the next morning my lawyer called me. It was Al Davis, who by then was the third lawyer working on my case along with Bierbower and Sharp.

"Hey, Jeb," he asked, "how are you?"

"Okay," I answered. He knew as well as I did that it wasn't a great question, but there aren't any better ones you can ask a man in prison. So both of us were being patient with the other.

"I'm afraid I've got some bad news for you, Jeb," Al announced.

I thought he must have seen the interview, too.

"What is it?" I asked.

"Well—I just had a call from Judge Sirica's office," he said. This wasn't like Al. Usually he didn't waste time. He'd just tell me what was happening. Now he seemed to be stalling.

"He says you can go home," he said.

"What do you mean?" I asked. Of course, he had been stalling. He knew what a shock this would be.

"You're free, Jeb. The judge just released you. He thinks you've served enough time."

Finally Al's words were beginning to make sense. "You mean a parole?"

"No-o-o. Not a parole." Al explained. "Not probation, either. He just let you go. You, Dean, Kalmbach. Jeb—go home. Call Gail and tell her to come and get you. Do you understand me? *Get outta there!"*

It was eleven o'clock in the morning. I called home but no one answered. I waited and called again, but still no answer. Then I called Louie Evans. When I told him what had happened, he exulted, "Then this is the way the Lord wants it to be, Jeb. It's wonderful!"

"I can't reach Gail," I told him. "She isn't home."

"Don't worry," Louie assured me. "We'll find her. I'll come out there with her and get you—as soon as possible."

I looked around for Herb Kalmbach, but learned that he was at the prosecutors' that morning. So was Chuck Colson. I was sorry about Chuck. He was the only one of us who would be staying behind, and that would be painful. It was ironic as well, because the judge who sentenced Chuck was supposed to be so much more reasonable than Sirica. I prayed that it wouldn't be long before Chuck was a free man, too. Fortunately, a few weeks later Judge Gesell released Chuck under conditions similar to ours.

John Dean already knew. His lawyers had called him earlier and he was getting ready to leave for California, where his wife was waiting for him.

I kept trying to reach Gail, but she wasn't home. Finally, around 2 P.M., I got Stuart, who had just come home from school.

"Hi, daddy!" he said, surprised and pleased by my call.

"Hi, Stu," I said. "Is mommy there?"

"No, she isn't," he answered. "I'm the only one here."

I knew Gail would arrive soon because she didn't like the children to come home to an empty house.

This was going to be difficult. Stuart was only

seven, and what I had to tell him didn't seem to make sense to me, either.

"Stuart," I began, "when mommy comes home, tell her to come to prison and get me and bring me home."

"But, daddy," Stuart said, "how can you come home? They won't let you do that."

"Yes, they will, Stuart. The judge said I can go home now. It's all right. Just tell mommy to come and get me."

"You mean you can come home for good? You can stay, and you don't have to go back to prison?"

"That's right, Stu. I can come home for good."

He understood then, and so did I.

Some time later, Gail met the judge at a prayer breakfast and thanked him for what he had done.

"Well," he said. "I just thought it was about time for Jeb to return to his family." People who knew him well had commented on his awareness of the suffering inflicted on the families of those who were sent to prison, and I think his remark to Gail only confirms that sensitivity in him.

I hadn't known it at the time, but about a month before I was released, Senator Mark Hatfield wrote a most eloquent letter to Judge Sirica. More than anything I have ever read, it embodies the principles of covenant love I have come to know through my Christian brothers and sisters:

... I barely knew Mr. Magruder during the time he served in government, and have only become deeply related to him and his family since the time of his sentencing. This has occurred through a church fellowship group in which we became acquainted after our wives became mutual participants. Thus I write you on this matter purely out of a personal knowledge and relationship with the Magruder family, and not because of any past political cooperation between us which, to be frank, never existed.

From my personal experience, it is evident to me that the suffering imposed on Mr. Magruder and his family is far more severe than could be originally anticipated. You are probably aware that Mr. Magruder is the only Watergate defendant with a young family: his children are Whitney, 14, Justin, 12, Tracy, 10, and Stuart, 7. The deprivation of their father for the past several months has left its toll. Furthermore, each time Mr. Magruder is called to testify, the strain from public exposure to his family becomes greater.

But far more important than these factors, which are to some extent the unfortunate consequences of any prison sentence, is the personal and spiritual development, brought about by a searching inward examination, on the part of Mr. Magruder himself. I can personally attest to you that Jeb Magruder has undergone a total reevaluation of his values and commitments, as an individual, because of his wrongdoing in the Watergate conspiracy. Mr. Magruder's minister, Reverend Louis Evans of the National Presbyterian Church, who travels to meet with him each Friday, and to share together deeply in such matters, can likewise convey the contrition, inner growth, and personal transformation taking place in his life.

. . . It seems clear beyond any doubt to me that the purpose of Mr. Magruder's criminal sentencing, as far as motivating him to come to understand his debt to society and to pay the cost of his breaches of the law, has been fully served. . . .

. . . You are aware, I am sure, that I have never countenanced the injustices perpetrated on this nation by the Administration of our former President. Firmly, I believe that full justice must be done to all cases, in order for the respect of law to be strengthened throughout our nation. But just as firmly, I believe that full justice has been served in the case of Jeb Magruder. The dictates of compassion, allowed within our system of criminal justice, would indicate, in my judgment, that Mr. Magruder, having fully confessed his guilt and paid a deep and searing personal cost for his crime, now be allowed to fulfill his desire to serve the needs of others, and the good of society and humanity. . . .

The Senator didn't have to write that letter. In fact, for a Republican member of Congress to speak up for me at that time was a political risk. But I don't think the Senator was thinking in terms of politics or party or risks. He was just being a Christian brother.

When a man leaves prison, it is customary for him to give his fellow prisoners some of his possessions. There wasn't much I could give to the other men besides my radio and a few books and shelves. They already had all the clothes they needed. They had enough money to buy little extras, and they ate very well. What they didn't have was my sudden freedom, which only made them more aware of their confinement. But they gave me a good sendoff.

"Keep running," Skitch said as he put his massive hand in mine and shook it briefly.

"You, too," I said. "I'll keep in touch."

"Sure," Skitch replied, but there was a tone in his voice that told me he had heard those words before.

"I mean it, Skitch," I assured him. "My letters might bore you to tears, but I'm going to write them anyway."

"Okay," Skitch answered, and he half smiled. "I might even write you back."

The other men went inside as we drove away. But Skitch stood there until we were out of sight.

11

On the Outside

HEY, JEB, GOOD to have you back," the call would begin.

"Good to be here," I'd say.

"Listen, we're having a little get-together at our house Saturday night—and we want you and Gail to come. How about it?"

"Thanks—but, no, I don't think so."

"You doing something else?"

"No, that isn't it."

"Jeb, we understand. But it's all over. You're back home—and a little fun is just what you need."

"Maybe—but we're not up to it. Thanks, anyway."

And then there was the silence of disappointment. I could hear it as clearly as words. The caller was taking my refusal personally and felt I was rejecting him. It wasn't that at all—yet I couldn't explain what it was, either. There were many calls like that, some from people who had stood by us and some from acquaintances who had backed away and now felt it was safe to approach us again. Most of them thought that since Gail and I looked okay, we were okay. Prison was over, done with, and now it was time to get back to being the way we were. But that was impossible. We could never go back because prison and everything else we had experienced had changed us—maybe not on the outside, but certainly inside. We weren't ready to laugh and have fun. We were exhausted.

Grateful as we were for the release, it had come so suddenly we couldn't prepare for it. One day I had been a prisoner, the next day I was free, back home, a father and husband again. That was something of a shock, but it was hard to explain it to people in a way they could understand.

Of course, with some people we didn't have to explain. Louie Evans, for one—"I'm here if you need me, Jeb," he said when he left for home the night he and Gail brought me back from Holabird. "But don't feel you *have* to need me." In other words, he was telling me he wasn't expecting a lot of attention now, because he was my friend. He was just there, unconditionally, whether I needed him or not.

One of the odd things about coming back home from prison is that you lose some of the friends who saw you through the rough times. Some of them feel that now you ought to spend a lot of time with them, and when they find out that the only thing you want to do is be by yourself, with your family, the friendship dies. I don't think I would have understood that, before. I used to think friendship was friendship, that's all. But now I realize that there are different kinds of friendship, almost as many kinds as there are people.

It hurts to lose some of those friends, because we love them, and we will always be grateful for everything they did for us. And we are sorry we couldn't just put prison behind us and have a good time again. It would have been pleasant, but we weren't up to it. I understand why some friends felt the way they did because, frankly, I had some of those same expectations myself. It took some time for me to realize that maybe a person never gets over being in prison.

For months after I was released, I used to wake up at night and think I was back in Holabird or Allenwood. I'd lie there in the dark and listen for the familiar sounds of other men sleeping or tossing or walking around. Then, finally, I would realize I was home. The experience was the reverse of the one I had when I first went to Allenwood. It still happens now and then.

I never used to cry, but now I cry easily and sometimes unexpectedly. Maybe it's a carryover from the depression a prisoner feels, or maybe it's because I'm more sensitive than I used to be. Probably it's both. But sometimes a thought, a word, or a feeling hits me and the tears roll down my cheeks. If that had happened a few years ago, when I thought it was unmanly to cry, I don't think I could have handled it. Now I accept it as part of being human. In fact, it's good to feel things deeply, even when they hurt.

I don't laugh as easily because things that used to be funny don't seem funny anymore. People tell me I used to be gregarious, and I suppose I would agree with that, but I'm not that way anymore. Socially I don't feel part of the group now. I enjoy being with people, but I seem to be more of an observer than a participant. I don't know why.

And yet there is a new capacity to get closer to friends on a one-to-one basis, to talk about some of the mysteries of life and try to puzzle them out.

What happens to people matters much more to me now than it ever did before.

I've kept in touch with Skitch, and he answers most of my letters. When Holabird closed down he was transferred to a heavy prison in the Southwest, which is exactly what he thought would happen. And, as he also expected, his wife broke under the strain of the separation and filed suit for divorce. I think Skitch would rather die than admit any feelings about it, but I know that hurt him. He's taking a correspondence course in air conditioning repairs, and he says he'll look us up when he gets out. I hope he does. The best news from Skitch was the Christmas card he sent us—there was a nativity scene on the cover.

One of the uncomfortable things about having been in prison is that you're a sitting duck, especially if your name is in the newspapers. People can say just about anything they want about you and get away with it. It happened to me only a few weeks after I was released. A new book by Jimmy Breslin was published at that time and in it he had written a fascinating little anecdote involving me— fascinating, but totally untrue. His source, he said, was Congressman Tip O'Neill, who heard it from Congressman Peter Rodino, who in turn heard it from someone else, supposedly who heard it from Cornelius Gallagher, the former New Jersey Congressman who was in Allenwood at the same time I was. Gallagher, it seems, told someone else—who then told Rodino, who then told O'Neill, who then told Breslin—that on my first day at Allenwood he and I played tennis, and during the game I suggested he might know of some damaging information about Peter Rodino, who was also from New Jersey and was at that time heading the House Judiciary Committee looking into the grounds for a

Nixon impeachment. Breslin claimed that Gallagher said I told him the President would be grateful if he could come up with something, and hinted at a possible pardon. Well, since it was the best story in Breslin's book, it was excerpted in newspapers and magazines. *Here we go again,* I thought, and called my lawyer.

"I think it's a plain case of libel," I told Jim Sharp. "On my first day in Allenwood I couldn't have lifted a tennis racket with my two hands," I said. "And I didn't even meet Gallagher until I was there a few days."

"Did you talk politics?" Jim asked.

"Sure, we had that in common. But we just talked generally—nothing specific. Certainly not about the Judiciary Committee hearings in the context of Breslin's story." I added that the story was particularly ridiculous because I'd had no contact with Nixon since the Inaugural in January 1973. Certainly I wasn't one of his confidants.

Jim was silent.

"Look," I continued, "Breslin didn't ask me about this. He didn't even ask Gallagher to confirm it."

"Well, Breslin can say he believed the story to be accurate, and was assured it was, and so he printed it. That's his leg to stand on."

"What about mine?" I asked.

"You lost it when you went to prison, Jeb," Jim went on. "I hate to say it like this, but that's the way it is. You're a convicted felon and Breslin isn't, so whose word do you think a court would believe?"

I thought about that for a moment and realized Jim was advising me to expect other incidents of the same kind.

"Well, here's the way I think it must have happened," I explained. "Gallagher might have said something to a visitor about Magruder being at Allenwood and maybe they could work out some kind of a deal. He'd been in prison for a long time by then, and, like most of the other prisoners, he probably thought I still had some strings tied to the White House. Obviously, if he had read the tape transcripts he would have realized that I wasn't Number One on Nixon's Hit Parade. But then, the visitor must have passed on the comment, and by the time it got to Breslin it was a whole other story. Couldn't I make that clear, Jim? A press conference, maybe?"

"Jeb, you won't kill it that way," Jim assured me. "You'll only keep it alive."

He was right, and I knew that before I made the suggestion. It's just that it was hard to take Breslin's accusation without fighting back.

"Okay," I said grudgingly. "We'll forget it—or try to."

"Good," Jim said. "'Cause you've got to deal with your other problems. People have come out of the woodwork with suits against you."

"I know."

One suit was brought against me and everyone else involved in Watergate—from Nixon on down—by Larry O'Brien and the Democratic National Committee. It was a civil suit seeking damages, and it seemed to me to be absolutely legitimate. The Committee to Reelect ended up paying $600,000 in damages. Then a man named Spencer Oliver, whose phone had been bugged (mistakenly) in the Democratic Committee headquarters in the Watergate, pulled out of the group suit and filed one of his own against all of us. After that, James McCord sued me, and then the Cubans who had committed the burglary sued everyone. Even Jack Anderson, the columnist, sued. As my lawyers explained it to me, most of these people were not out to get money from me—and I certainly didn't have much to give. But the simplest way for them to get me into court to give testimony was to name me in a suit. That meant I had to appear for a deposition and sometimes had to appear in court to give evidence supporting the claims of the person filing the suit.

But when was it going to stop? As the list grew, the claims became more ridiculous.

"Here's a beauty," Bierbower told me. "A couple on the West Coast have filed suit against all you Watergate guys, claiming that they were being harassed by the police."

"That's crazy!" I protested. "How does that tie in with Watergate?"

"That's the part that's hard to figure out," Jim continued. "They claim that you could have controlled the police, and could have prevented the harassment—or maybe that you even instigated it. My guess is that this one will be thrown out of court on the first day."

"But meanwhile I still have to file a response and go through the whole story again, right?"

"Right. You know the routine."

I also knew these suits could cost me a bundle in legal fees—and travel expenses, because sometimes I would have to go halfway across the country to testify.

"Be patient, Jeb," Jim advised me. "It takes time to fade out of the spotlight."

How long? I wondered. The suits against me at that point totaled thirteen.

The way I was living wasn't helping me to fade out of the spotlight. When I look back now, I almost can't believe what I did. The very next day after getting out of Holabird, I started running as fast as ever, talking on the phone all day, agreeing to interviews and TV appearances, planning to write another book and signing up with a lecture bureau that wanted to send me to the college campuses. I was all over the place.

The truth is, I was scared. The money I had put aside to support Gail and the children was almost gone, and the thought of being broke always spurred me into action. And, as usual, when I was scared, my judgment was affected, so I made some stupid mistakes.

The worst mistake was that I went right back to relying on myself instead of trusting Christ to shape my life. There I was, assuming I could handle an emergency better than he could—and making a mess of it. What Gail and the children and I needed more than anything else was time to be together, to find out who we were and what had happened to our relationships during the months we were separated. Gail and I took a few days off in Puerto Rico, but that wasn't enough. Then I was off and running, hardly ever home.

I knew I would have a hard time finding a job. The big corporations weren't touching any of the Watergate people, and unless we had friends who could put in a good word for us, we were in trouble. I had a few good friends like that, so there was a chance I might have a few job offers sometime in the future. But when? I wasn't sure, either, that I wanted to go in that direction. I needed time—time to find out what God wanted me to do. So I was trying to buy some time by running fast.

My lecture agent was the American Program Bureau. Bob Walker, the president, did an excellent job. Within a few weeks I was booked into several colleges. The tour was frantic, but I enjoyed talking to college kids. They asked some tough, penetrating questions, but they were willing to listen to the answers. I found them to be extremely well informed and concerned about their world.

My first book, *An American Life*, was just coming out in paperback, and I had promised the publisher that I would go on a four-to-six-week publicity tour. It was the last thing in the world I needed, but the publisher was putting a lot of effort into making the book a success and I wanted to cooperate. At the time I agreed, I didn't realize how exhausting my life was going to be.

The publicity tour was rough. The press was skeptical of my conversion, not because they were anti-Christian but because most of them didn't understand what Christianity was all about. Like many other people, some of the reporters interpreted being a Christian with being a perfect human being, and since I obviously was far from perfect, they looked upon me as a hypocrite, or worse. In city after city, during interviews and press conferences, the questions were not about the book, but about my faith. And usually they were variations of the same basic concern:

"How can you claim to be a Christian after committing such a terrible crime?" Most of the reporters did not understand redemption, salvation, or forgiveness, and that was not the time for me to try to explain it all to them, either.

Another question often asked was the same one all the Watergate men were asked when they appeared in public: "How can you justify making money from what you did?" I tried to answer that one the way most of the other men did. "I've paid my debt to society," I would explain, "and now I have the same right to make a living that you do." Usually it didn't satisfy the questioners, most of whom seemed to want to hear me confess that I was guilty of committing a crime. Well, I had been confessing for a couple of years, and I felt it was time to go beyond that.

I was miserable out on the road. Gail and the children needed me at home and I needed them. I wanted to sit quietly and find out where I was and where I ought to be going. But there I was, caught up in all the things I had learned weren't important in life, while the important things were starving for attention. The idea of buying time may have seemed valid, but it wasn't working out—not when it meant putting off the things that counted. By the time I got around to them, maybe they wouldn't be there.

I was in Minneapolis on the third week of the publicity tour when I began to slow down and wonder why I was running at all. I remembered a prayer by John Baillie I had read in prison:

> O Thou who wast, and art, and art to come, I thank Thee that this Christian way whereon I walk is no untried or uncharted road, but a road beaten hard by the footsteps of saints, apostles, prophets and martyrs. I thank Thee for the finger posts and the danger signals with which it is marked at every turning, and which may be known to me through the study of the Bible, and of all history, and of all the great literature of the world.

The finger posts and danger signals were all around me, and it was time for me to take note of them. This road I was trying to walk was beaten hard by men and women who trusted Christ to guide them in *every* situation in life—not just whenever it was convenient. God was telling me something: study was what I needed, and I couldn't study while I was running in circles.

Then there was another interview and the usual question.

"How can you claim to be a Christian after what you did?" the young reporter asked, shaking his head in disapproval.

I knew then that I was wasting my time trying to answer, because he wouldn't be listening, anyway. In fact, the whole tour was a waste of time because there were other things I really had to do.

"Write whatever you want," I replied. "I don't think anything I say will change your mind."

I left the room and went back to my hotel where I put in a call to the publisher's promotion department. "I've had it, Barbara," I said. "I've done half the tour, and that's all I can do. I'm going home."

I took the first plane out. As we left the ground I felt myself relax. I was letting go of my confusion and giving it to Christ, which I should have done a long time ago. And by the time we touched down in Washington many things were becoming clear.

First of all, I didn't want to forget I had been in prison. Not that I wanted to dwell on it or let myself become depressed by memories of its dehumanization and loneliness. But God had been there with me. He had opened me up to so many insights I never would have had, and now I wanted to find out why. I was certain he wanted me to get something out of that experience, and if I tried to put it all behind me, then I would be turning my back on something extremely important that God had done in my life.

Soon after I was released from prison, I met Art De Moss, a leading Christian businessman who runs a large insurance company in Philadelphia. "Corky" Campbell, a Washington businessman and a Young Life board member, introduced us. Art was very supportive and understood my desire to use my experience. At first he helped me interview a number of companies.

But after much thought I realized I really didn't want to go back into the business world—at least, not yet. In Elton Trueblood's book, *The Essence of Spiritual Religion,* he said, "If we could see our daily tasks as part of the ministry, if we could know that what we do is valuable only as it helps in some way to arouse the sense of God's presence, then all life would be infinitely raised." I wanted to arouse that "sense of God's presence" through whatever I did for a living.

Then, too, I needed Christian nurture. What I really wanted were some seminary courses in Scripture and in the historical background of the Bible. That is the way my mind works—I need a complete examination of a subject. I have to explore it from every angle, and the deeper the exploration, the better. But, of course, I couldn't simply ignore my responsibilities and go into seminary.

So there had to be another way.

I felt strongly that God was telling me to look for an opening in a Christian service organization where I could put my skills to good use and at the same time do something God wanted done. Perhaps I could get into one of the prison reform groups. But the more I thought about that, the more I felt it wasn't where God wanted me. There were several prison reform groups, and they were doing as good a job as they could. But the prison system was so corrupt, and there was so little public indignation over its abuses, that little could be accomplished by an outside group. Even within the system there were some who had the best of intentions but seemed unable to carry them out. It wasn't unusual for a warden to be a former inmate, a man who knew what was wrong from the inside and who wanted to dedicate his life to correcting it. But sooner or later the system itself overwhelmed the man and he became as mute as the other reformers.

As for the prison ministries, they didn't really need someone like me, whose field is administration. I also thought I wouldn't be a very effective minister to prisoners because I was too conscious of the obstacles to their rehabilitation.

I had been doing some work as a consultant to a few Christian organizations, and some of them were interested in having me work for them full time.

Soon after my release from prison, and because of my background in mass marketing, I was asked by

Bill Bright to help on a new Campus Crusade for Christ program called "Here's Life, America." I worked with Bruce Cook, one of the finest men I've ever known. I would have enjoyed taking the program a few steps further, except that it required more travel than I thought I could handle. Through Bruce I was able to spend considerable time with Howard Hendricks, a professor at Dallas Theological Seminary, whose insights into Christianity, particularly as it relates to leadership and motivation were very helpful to me.

But there was another problem with Christian service organizations, and that was their salary scale. It was unbelievably low. While I didn't expect to earn the kind of salary I could have made in the secular business world, I had to have enough to meet my family's basic needs, and the offers coming my way were far below the strictest budget we could work out. I think this may be one of the reasons why Christian organizations have such difficulty getting experienced, effective people.

Then, in March of 1975, two excellent job openings came along, one with World Vision and the other with Young Life. World Vision's board chairman was Dr. Dick Halverson, minister of Fourth Presbyterian Church in Bethesda, Maryland, one of the largest Presbyterian churches in the county. Dick, whom I did not know well but who really wanted to help, indicated they were organizing a famine relief program and wanted someone to direct it. The job was fascinating, the salary was realistic, and whoever was chosen certainly would know that he was arousing "a sense of God's presence" every hour of his working day. The only catch was that the job required a great deal of travel for long periods of time. And, to be perfectly honest, World Vision, led by Stan Mooneyham and Ted Engstrom, was so well organized already they didn't need me.

But Young Life was something else. Here was an organization that had grown so fast it was in serious need of administration. They realized it, too, and were in the process of reorganizing. What they required were exactly the skills and experience I had. With them, I would be making a contribution.

And there was more. The whole Young Life method and goal appealed to me. Their ministry was to young people, to all types of teenagers—leaders, followers, athletes, and troubled kids.

Ordinarily some kids can get into a lot of trouble. Most of the men I saw in prison started out that way, and by the time they were adults it was too late to do much in the way of rehabilitation because crime was their way of life. But if they could have been reached when they were younger, if they could have been introduced to Christ in a way that made him real to them, then the chances were good that they wouldn't have ended up behind bars at all.

Maybe that was where I could use my prison experience—by trying to reach kids before they get into trouble.

Mark Hatfield was a member of the Young Life Board of Directors, and he was the one who told me they were looking for someone experienced in administration and promotion. Then he put me in touch with Young Life's president, Bill Starr. That was the beginning of three very trying months.

After our initial conversations, the people at Young Life and I felt comfortable with each other. It seemed to me that this was definitely where God wanted me to go, and I was excited about the challenge of the job. But there were a few dissenters. More than one person voiced concern that contributions to Young Life would fall off if a convicted felon became a member of the organization—and Young Life depends more on many small contributions than on a few large ones. Some felt that the

amount of publicity I had been receiving would prevent me from doing my work effectively. So, while
many things seemed to be right about the job, it still
wasn't mine. No one said yes, and no one said no.
Every now and then I was called to the Young Life
headquarters in Colorado Springs for another interview, and I always was sent home with strong reas-
surances. But I knew that an internal debate was
going on, and the only thing I could do was wait and
let Jesus Christ work it out.

Waiting was never easy for me, and becoming a
Christian hadn't made me more patient. I guess the
old personality traits remain, at least for a long
time. I kept wanting to pick up the phone and call
Bill Starr and say, "Look, am I in or out? Tell me!"
Then another interesting job offer came through
from a group of Christian businessmen in Chicago.
The salary was good and the atmosphere was the
kind that encouraged a person to express his faith
through his work. Our family had lived in Chicago
years before and liked it there. Still, I had the feeling that God wanted me to go to Young Life, so I
said no, with many thanks, to the Chicago group, and
went on waiting for a call from Colorado Springs.

There were things to do while I waited. Gail and I
had a life to rebuild and much to learn about each
other. Becoming a Christian doesn't necessarily
make a marriage easier because a husband and wife
are far more aware of their shortcomings than they
were before. Or, rather, they no longer accept those
shortcomings as the natural state of a marriage.
They know now how good it can be and how far
they are from that goal. Gail and I had to go
through some painful groping. I was defensive about
being a good provider because I was unemployed.
Gail was close to that time in life when a woman's
children grow up and go away, and she was aware
that she had to find new interests and challenges.

Children change almost every day, and coming home to mine after a seven months' absence made me feel I had to become reacquainted with them. They had matured so much! Whitney, going on fifteen, was unusually mature for his age and very stable. I think he set an example for the others and helped to hold things together while I was in prison. Justin and Tracy were so good-natured that they created a harmonious atmosphere for the whole family. Stuart, strong-willed and bright, was the only one with obvious scars from the prison experience, probably because he had been too young to understand why it happened. He seemed to be afraid I would have to leave him again, and every time I had to go away from home—which, unfortunately, had been happening too often—he would say, "Daddy, do you have to go back to prison now?" He had trouble sleeping, too, and there were some bad dreams.

I had always tried to spend as much time as I could with our children, not only because I was trying to do what was right, but because I enjoyed them. Now I enjoyed them even more because they were reaching an age where they had more things to discuss with a father—cars, bikes, sports, trips—and I was just glad to be around. I remembered what I had learned in prison, that God, Gail, the kids, and the work God wanted me to do were the really important things in life. For a few months I had forgotten—again the old habits taking over—but I asked Christ to help me remember more clearly in the future.

Finally, on a sunny, pleasant afternoon in May, the phone rang. It was Bill Starr calling.

"Welcome to Young Life, Jeb," he said. "When can you start?"

"Is right away too soon?" I asked.

Bill laughed. "That's fine, Jeb. Sorry we kept you waiting so long."

Now that the period of anxiety was over, I saw how many other things were right about my new career. Besides arousing a sense of God's presence through my work, I would also have the opportunity to take seminary courses. In fact, every new staff member at Young Life is required to take graduate study courses leading to an M.A. in Youth Ministries. The courses are offered by the Institute of Youth Ministries, a joint program with Fuller Seminary, which is one of the places I would have wanted to go if I'd had my choice. Then there was the location. We needed to get away from Washington, where we were too well-known and there were too many unpleasant associations. Going with Young Life meant moving to Colorado Springs, which was what we needed. It's a lovely town in an incredibly beautiful setting rich with opportunities for outdoor activities. The children would love it! And that was important, because one of the sad aspects of leaving Washington was the fact that our children would miss the many good friends they had there. Being able to ski, hike, and do just about anything they wanted to do outdoors wasn't a substitute for good friends, but it would be something exciting to do and help them make new friends.

Another advantage was the cost of living in Colorado Springs, which was quite a bit lower than Washington. By careful budgeting, we would get by.

It felt so good to be able to tell Dick Halverson, Louie, Gene Arnold, Doug Coe, Harold Hughes, Mark Hatfield, and all my covenant brothers that I had a job. I knew they were as anxious about my future as I was. They had shared my confusion and indecision. They had supported me when I decided to let God make the decisions for me, and when nothing happened for the longest time they kept on supporting me. Now I knew where I was going—and it was where God wanted me to be.

12

Young Life

A FEW MONTHS AGO I was visiting a Young Life club in Pittsburgh. Another staff member and I were standing in a church basement, watching a group of boys working on several Honda motorcycles. The bikes were provided by Young Life. Each one "belonged" to a few boys who took turns riding it and keeping it in absolutely beautiful condition.

"See that kid over there," the staff member said, pointing to a small boy who couldn't have been more than twelve years old.

I nodded.

"Well, he used to be one of the most notorious shoplifters in Pittsburgh," he told me.

And there he was, too interested in working on his

bike to think about stealing. Sure, it had been the bike that attracted him to Young Life, but he kept coming back because something else had hold of him now. He was interested in Jesus Christ. Why? Because the Young Life leader had made Christ real to him.

Young Life began in a small town in Texas back in 1938 when a minister decided that there was no use waiting for young people to come to church— the church had to go out and reach them. So the minister hired a young seminary student named Jim Rayburn, and said, "Jim, I want you to go out there where the kids are and get something started!" He wasn't quite sure what he meant by "get something started," and neither was Jim Rayburn. But both men realized that many teenagers knew almost nothing about Jesus Christ, and what little they did know made Christ seem abstract and distant. Something had to be done about that.

Rayburn began by simply talking to kids. He met them on their own ground where they were more comfortable, which meant he spent a great deal of time in school yards and classrooms. Knowing that kids like to be together with their friends, he got the idea for a club which he called "Young Life." He knew he couldn't just stand up and preach about Jesus Christ; the kids had heard such words before. Instead, he would love them in the manner that Christ loved them—unconditionally. Through his relationship with them he could show them what Christ was like. He would be a friend, a leader to whom they could look for guidance, a confidant who would listen and not judge. Then, when he knew them well, when he had a place in their lives, he would have earned the right to talk to them about Jesus Christ, and the words would mean something. Once kids experienced Christian friendship in human terms, they could go on to the spiritual level.

It worked. Before the year was out, Jim Rayburn was training other youth pastors in the Young Life method so that more clubs could be started. Then there were weekend and summer camps where young people could spend some of the happiest hours of their lives.

Today Young Life is an international organization that reaches as many as 200,000 kids each year through its clubs. Sixteen thousand enjoy the summer camps, and 75,000 attend weekend camps.

The Young Life method—they call it "incarnational theology"—appealed to me because it reminded me of the way my Christian friends in Washington had introduced me to Christ. Instead of telling me about him, they related to me in a Christ-like manner until I understood that if they could love me deeply, then so could Christ. This is the way the Scriptures tell us Jesus Christ himself worked. He didn't give a speech and then dash off to another engagement. Jesus developed relationships with people on an individual basis. He took the time to dine with Zaccheus; he was a friend of Lazarus, Mary, Martha, and so many others. Taking his disciples into his life, he entered theirs.

From my first day with Young Life I was very busy and happy to be that way, especially after the months of idleness. We had a fine, big, old house which Gail was making into a home for us, and Colorado Springs was a good place to live.

I hadn't anticipated the amount of traveling I would have to do, and that was a little disturbing. But I was so happy to be accepted as a Young Life staff member that I found it hard to turn down an invitation to attend a banquet and talk about what we were trying to accomplish. So, almost immediately I was caught up in a whirl of one-night stands that took me back and forth through the entire evangelical community.

I had other problems, too. Shortly after I joined Young Life and moved to Colorado Springs, the IRS informed me that they were going to audit my 1972 tax return—no doubt because of my Watergate involvements. They did what they call a "gross receipts" test, which means that the auditors go back over the taxpayer's income for a given year and compare that to his expenses. If there is a sizeable difference, they suspect—and assume—fraud. My accountant and I must have spent at least three weeks going over my records. Some twenty people at IRS—including a special criminal investigation team—were also involved.

I think this shows the type of harassment one goes through when the "authorities" get on your trail. It was a full court press of all my activities, checking bank records and stock brokerage accounts in Washington and other cities, and so on.

In the course of their investigation, the IRS turned up a check for $375.00 forged in my name by a woman from Urbana, Illinois. They tried to connect me with her, but couldn't. Finally, after a year of scrutiny, they found a mistake in my arithmetic: I still owed the government $31.00! I can't even begin to estimate how much of other taxpayers' money it cost to find that error.

As a new Christian I had some difficulties. I expected all other Christians to be perfect creatures, which, of course, they aren't. So I was dismayed to find that even in the midst of the Christian community there are rivalries among those who want to introduce Jesus Christ to those who do not know him. And there are some in the Christian community who are absolutely certain that their understanding of the gospel is the *only* correct interpretation and that all others are blasphemies. And then there are those who say that certain things are "God's will," when they are really referring to their own will. There are those, too, who are determined to reach their evangelistic goals no matter who gets hurt.

Some claim that their affluence comes from God —and I suppose there is nothing wrong with that. But when the other side of that coin implies that poverty is a result of sin, and therefore not deserving of compassion, I have trouble agreeing. It smacks of "the rich are good and the poor are bad," and I know that isn't true. While some instances of poverty may indeed be a result of sin, many are the result of economic policies over which the poor have no control. And I also know of many instances in which great wealth is not being put to any good use.

But Christians, like everyone else, are human. They have their flaws, their weaknesses and failures. Until I understood that, I was impatient with some of my associates and perhaps a little frightened that I, too, was going to be less than perfect, no matter how long I had been a Christian. Then one day Louie Evans called to see how I was getting along and I blurted out all my frustrations to him.

"You're absolutely right, Jeb," Louie told me. "None of us is perfect, and we aren't ever going to be, either."

"Well, let's not use the word 'perfect,' then," I replied impatiently. "What I mean is that I'm seeing some of the same qualities I saw in the secular business world—ambition, pride, jealousy. I hate to say this, but there's even some dishonesty."

"Of course, there is," Louie said. "Maybe even a lot."

"That's hard for me to take, Louie," I went on. "I know you could say, Who am I to be so high and mighty about a little falsehood now and then? But that's just the trouble. I *know* where it can lead. I used to make the same little excuses to myself, and that's how a thing like Watergate can happen."

"I can understand that, Jeb," Louie countered. "But maybe you have to try to be more patient. You know, I think there is a fundamental difference between a Christian and a non-Christian, and maybe it's this: Both of them are at the bottom of the barrel, but the Christian is trying to crawl up and out. He's never going to make it all the way, but the important thing is for him to keep on trying."

It was just like Louie not to tell me that I was being judgmental, which I was. I recalled my anger at the reporter who expected Christians to be flawless, and yet I wasn't far from having the same attitude. What could I say in the face of that realization?

"Thanks, Louie," I said. "Thanks again."

Louie chuckled. "I just thought of a funny little card someone gave Colleen the other day. It said, 'Please be patient—God isn't finished with me yet.' I guess we all could use one of those."

"Especially me," I said.

"Jeb, the thing that concerns me is that maybe you're getting out front too much," Louie added. "I mean, you're still a young Christian."

It was amazing how he sensed the vague uneasiness that had begun to form inside me. "Well, I didn't mind at first," I told him. "In fact, I was glad to be doing something constructive. But I find that when I take on these speaking engagements, I don't get much of a chance to talk about anything except Watergate and my testimony. That's what people keep asking me about."

"I thought that might happen," Louie said. "In a sense, Jeb, you're a celebrity, whether you like it or not. And people like to hear the repentant sinner."

"That's okay, as long as it does some good."

"I'm sure it does," Louie said. "Probably you can relate to some people better than anyone else can, and in that sense it's a ministry. But what about you? Are you getting any Christian nurture from it?"

I thought of the hectic schedules I was keeping wherever I spoke. No matter how hard I tried to keep the pace reasonable, appointment piled upon appointment until faces became a blur of anonymity. "Would you believe it?" I told Louie. "In the midst of all those people, I get lonely."

"I do believe it. You can't have any Christian fellowship that way."

How right he was. Wherever I went, my hosts were under pressure to "ask Jeb to say a few words" to one group after another. Their intentions were good, but by accepting in my behalf they literally cut me off from close contact with anyone around me. I barely had time to shake hands. And I felt uncomfortable about refusing to fulfill those commitments, so I did my best to keep them all.

Don't get me wrong. I wanted to talk about Jesus Christ and the way he had changed my life. If I could help to bring him into another person's heart, I was grateful for the opportunity. But the more I raced through the banquet circuit, the more I questioned whether that goal was being accomplished in any sense at all. By giving my testimony I could, perhaps, demonstrate the power of Jesus Christ to love and forgive and save, but I wasn't all that sure I was bringing him closer to anyone. And if I was, what happened to that person the next day when I was off and running to another engagement?

It seemed to me that meeting Christ was one thing, and learning how to live his way was another, and you couldn't accomplish both in a matter of a few minutes. I learned so much about Christ through relationships, and relationships take time.

After my conversation with Louie I did some thinking. I remembered some of the other Christian "celebrities" I had met along the banquet circuit. Some of them were cynical, which puzzled me. They seemed to have lost their zest in talking about Christ, not only in public, but privately. A few of them confided that they had expected their Christian experience to be much deeper than it was—that something was missing, and they weren't sure what it was.

Remarks like those used to make me uncomfortable, and now finally I understood them. It was because they touched off a sense of alarm within me. I was afraid I was going to lose something, something that meant more to me than anything else in the world. Did it have to be this way? Did new Christians have to become objects applauded from a distance rather than brothers and sisters sharing the warmth of God's love with each other?

I wasn't able to search for an answer to those questions then because it was summer and time for me to begin my theology courses at our Institute in Colorado Springs. For eight weeks there were no banquets, no trips and even very little time in the office. I spent my days in classrooms, and my afternoons and evenings—sometimes late into the night —learning about the Old and New Testaments. Our professors were outstanding, and the courses were difficult. I enjoyed every demanding minute of those days, and when I finished with straight A's I felt it was an important accomplishment. At last I was beginning to understand something about the words I was using at all those banquets.

"Salvation," "forgiveness," "personal relation-

ship with Jesus Christ"—mention these words at
any Christian gathering and you get an immediate,
warm response from your audience. But can we
really understand what these words mean simply by
hearing them so many times? I don't think we can
understand them in a moment or through constant
repetition. It takes a lifetime at the feet of Christ to
understand and—more importantly—*to live them.*

But it was fall and time to get going again, so
there I was, trying to cut down my schedule—yet
watching it become busier and busier each week. I
was running again. Though I was doing it in Christian circles, nevertheless I was running. And I knew
that wasn't what God wanted me to do.

I thought I remembered reading something in
Colleen Evans' book, *A New Joy,* that described my
feelings, and I glanced through its pages until I
found the passage.

Colleen was describing one morning when she
woke up and found that the "glow" in her life was
gone:

> For several years before I married Louie, I had
> worked in the motion picture industry.... During
> those years I also became a very enthusiastic believer
> in Jesus Christ. To me it didn't seem unusual that a
> spiritual rebirth should happen to someone in my pro-
> fession—I have known, and still know, many dedi-
> cated Christians in the motion picture industry. But to
> many people the combination of my belief and my
> profession had a special attraction. Because of that I
> was often asked to speak to various groups, telling
> them how Christ came into my life. Even after I left
> my motion picture work for my "other career," the
> one I wanted more, the speaking invitations con-
> tinued.
>
> Because I have always been eager to share my faith,
> I said yes to as many requests as I could, although
> speaking was not then (and is not now) a thing I leap

toward with joy. Eventually the pressure became uncomfortable because I allowed myself to be influenced by a few people who felt that it was not only my opportunity but my duty to speak about Jesus publicly.

Yes, I could see where the glow had gone. It had retreated to deep inside me. I was beginning to feel like an "up front" Christian and obviously I was resisting the celebrity bit. It is one thing to talk about being a Christian in front of groups, but quite another to be a Christian in your home and in your community. I longed to be more deeply Christian where it really counted, but I needed help.

Colleen seemed to understand exactly what I was feeling. I knew that those who kept asking me for my testimony meant well, but they actually weren't doing well by me because one day I would wake up and the glow would be gone. Colleen Evans had to learn how to say no to all those requests so she could put more time into a deep study of the Bible and find out what it meant to *be* a Christian. And when she did that, the glow returned, brighter than ever.

"We must listen to Christ rather than to other Christians," someone had said. I wondered if I could find the courage to do that—and do it in a way that would not hurt other Christians.

I could speak publicly if I had to, and I had done a great deal of it in my life. But it wasn't my gift. Even though people said I seemed at ease in front of an audience, I really wasn't. I had trained myself to appear at ease, and that's a different thing. God had given me the gifts of administration and working with small groups, and I knew that was what I should be doing. I shouldn't be flying around the country, repeating words whose meaning I had only begun to understand. I should be sitting at my desk in my Young Life office, doing the coordinating and organizing work I was given the ability to do. And I should be spending as much time with my Bible and in a classroom as I possibly could.

It happened one day, just like that. God was telling me to go ahead and do what I knew he wanted me to do. He said I didn't have to travel the banquet circuit anymore. That had been my idea, not God's, anyway. My schedule was already filled for several weeks ahead, but I called in Ginger, my very capable assistant, and said, "I want you to cancel all my speaking engagements—all of them."

Immediately I felt tremendous relief. Wherever possible I would get in touch with those who had asked me to speak and try to explain why I couldn't. I prayed they would understand.

Then more pieces of my life began to fall into place.

Even before I came to Young Life I had realized that the experiences of Watergate and prison had wounded me emotionally. My vulnerability was not only acute, but very near the surface of my being, and it would take time for me to get my emotions under control again. That was one of the reasons why I didn't want to go back into the secular business world. The rough-and-tumble, sometimes brutal, competition might have destroyed me. A Christian organization—well, that would be different. Everyone would be working toward the same goals and with the same point of view.

At that time, however, Young Life was going through some turmoil of its own. Not only was it growing as an organization, but there were management changes and conflicting interpretations about where Young Life ought to be going.

So there I was in a management position with considerable responsibility and no awareness of the many different sensitivities surrounding me. On top of that, my job was to set up a communications program that had never been part of Young Life before, and one which would affect the working patterns of almost everyone in the organization. The program was very much needed by Young Life and, knowing how much it could increase the organization's efficiency, I was eager to get the job done. Perhaps too eager.

It wasn't long before I ran into an unexpected stumbling block: some people didn't want to change their work habits, and some didn't want to change so fast. My attempts to increase efficiency were producing tensions, and I didn't know how to handle them. Instead of looking at the problem objectively, I took it personally and emotionally. *Why couldn't we all go in the same direction and at the same pace,* I thought, *when it's so obvious what has to be done? After all, we're Christians!* I was confusing the human condition with the spiritual condition, assuming that since we all worshiped the same Lord, we should go about serving him in the same way.

Louie Evans had called me a "young" Christian. Actually I was an immature one.

Somehow, as God led me toward the kind of spiritual life that was best for me, I felt him opening me up to a new understanding of the conflicts in my work. I saw that Young Life had also been through a difficult experience and, like me, needed time to adjust to the changes that were taking place. And, yes, we all did serve the same Lord, but each of us had to do it in his or her own way. Those differences were created by God himself and were to be cherished, not resented. We still could become more efficient—which was important to our mission—but in good time. And with allowances for the fact that we are *Christian human beings.*

God was reordering my priorities. He was telling

me that getting the job done is not as important as how the job is done.

It was the beginning of my second summer with Young Life and time for another eight weeks at our Institute. I couldn't wait for classes to begin! This time the courses were even more difficult, and I worked harder than ever. But something deep inside me was beginning to respond to this kind of demand. I wasn't only getting an education; I honestly felt I was following God's will for my life.

I don't think there is any one way for us to recognize what is—or is not—God's will for each one of us. That's something that grows out of an individual's relationship with God, and so it may come in different ways to different men and women. In my case, I seem to recognize God's will by the way I respond to the things that are going on in my life. For instance, speaking at banquets was demotivating me, so I didn't feel that God was beckoning me to go farther in that direction. But studying—really studying—the deeper meaning of God's Word was the most exciting experience I had ever known. It felt right. It felt as if God were saying, "Jeb, this is where you belong."

Eight weeks once a year wasn't going to be enough. I needed more. I also wanted to work toward a Master of Divinity degree—Hebrew, Greek, and all. After that summer it became apparent that I should pursue this goal. It wasn't only the degree I wanted, but rather a more penetrating study of Scripture. This, I have found, gives me a deeper understanding of my relationship to Christ.

I decided to have a talk with Bob Mitchell, the president of Young Life. Bob had been with Young Life since its beginning in Dallas, Texas, and his father and uncle also had been early supporters.

Thus he knew the organization, its goals and its problems from one end to the other.

Bob and I had worked closely and had become good friends since I arrived in Colorado Springs. In fact, when my father passed away shortly after I joined Young Life, the first person I called was Bob. He and his wife, Claudia, came right to the hospital and later he conducted the service at my father's funeral. I thought he would understand what was happening in my life. He did. After I told him what I hoped to do, he agreed that I should take a leave of absence in order to attend Princeton Seminary in Princeton, New Jersey.

Consequently, I will enroll in Princeton in September, 1978. I considered Princeton because it offers a unique combination of courses in theology and psychology. While I work toward my Master of Divinity degree I can also take courses leading to a Master in Social Work in concert with Rutgers University. Eventually these studies will allow me to become involved in direct ministry or qualify me for secular accreditation as a therapist. Perhaps, then, I will get into some kind of counseling work. Whatever I do, I want to become involved with human need on a personal level.

This is my way of stepping out of the spotlight. I really don't feel I ever belonged there, and I hope those who know me will understand my reasons.

Jesus Christ has changed my life, but that change is still going on, and, hopefully, will continue for the rest of my life. He turned me in a new direction, but I don't believe he intends me to stand in one spot along the way. He wants me to move ahead.

I have a testimony to give, and I want most earnestly to give it. But I don't want to make a career of it, or allow that to become my entire Christian experience. The moment when I met Christ was the beginning of my life, and the rest of that life now has to be lived out as Christ chooses. When I talk about the moment I met Christ, I am referring to the past—which in itself is all right. But to speak over and over about a moment in the past prevents me from moving on into the future—and that is where I must go.

This is not a whim. It is a decision based on study of the Scriptures and obedience to what I believe to be God's instructions for me.

During the time I was looking about for an answer to the uneasiness within me, I found so much help from the letters of Paul. As I read and reread them, I realized that Paul could have given the greatest testimony of all time—and yet he didn't go around just talking about *it*. Perhaps he did privately, in moments of meaningful relatedness with others. But mostly he spoke about what must be done, not about what had been done, and about where Christianity was going. He was concerned with where God was leading him, not where he had been. In fact, after Paul met Christ on the Damascus Road, he made a few attempts at speaking and they didn't turn out too well. Then he disappeared for several years before he returned as a powerful force for Christ.

I can't help but wonder what Paul did during those years. We know about some of the places where he stayed, but much of the time is a mystery, something between him and God. Whatever it was, he was preparing for the work God wanted him to do.

I don't intend to disappear. I'm simply stepping out of the spotlight because I can't see very well in the glare of it. I don't think I am most effective for Christ there. I am meant for quieter pursuits, and it's time I accepted that truth.

My work is very important to me, but I'm learn-

ing to fit other things into my life. I read as much as
I can—mostly theological and psychological books,
but I still enjoy a good mystery story for relaxation.
I don't play as much tennis as I once did. I prefer
biking because it gives me a greater sense of physical freedom. I try to bike about sixteen miles four
mornings a week, and on weekends anywhere from
twenty-five to fifty miles. One weekend Mike Has-
sel, a Young Life friend, and I went ninety-six miles
in one day, and maybe some day we'll break that
record. Biking, to me, is more than a way to keep
fit; it offers me a form of spiritual nurture I find es-
sential to my well-being.

Rearranging my schedule has also given me a
chance to spend more time with my kids. We ski a
lot and sometimes go back-packing in the moun-
tains. Last summer we took a week off and went
down Colorado's Green River on a raft, a wonder-
fully exciting experience.

Some of my covenant brothers and I still keep in
touch, and occasionally we get to see each other.
They have a way of sensing when a note or a telephone call is just what I need. I'm also in a fellowship group with a few other Young Life people with
whom I've become close. Those men who work with
me at Young Life include Bill Taylor, Bill Kelly,
Jim Nordby, and Bill Russell. They have been both
covenant brothers and fellow workers.

Most former prisoners have a desire to see our
prison system reformed, and I'm no exception. As a
committed Christian I became especially aware of
the need for reform as I studied Paul's Epistles and
realized that he and many of the early apostles and
disciples spent much of their time in prison.

It would take a separate book to discuss the needs
for prison reform in our country, but it seems to me
that there are some fairly simple ways in which we

could treat criminals with some degree of humanity and at the same time avoid increasing the crime rate.

For example, many people who commit crimes could be punished without being sent to prison. Dr. Jim Benjamin, with whom I served time in Allenwood, could have served his time at a public health service hospital, where he could have paid constructively for what he had done. He also would not have been cut off from his family by spending his time in a prison four hours from his home.

Many other nonviolent, nonhabitual offenders could be sentenced to work for local charitable organizations so that their lives and those of their families would not be destroyed by the prison experience. Obviously, they also would be contributing something to society rather than adding to its tax burden.

Even some violent criminals might be spared the prison sentence. Over one-third of the violent crimes committed in our country are crimes of passion that occur during domestic quarrels, barroom fights, and similar situations. In most cases the persons committing these crimes probably will never commit another crime of this type—so wouldn't it make sense to sentence them to some kind of constructive service instead of sending them to a maximum-security prison? If we treat them like habitually violent criminals, then that is what they very likely will become. And we must accept the fact that nearly all criminals return to society—eventually.

In most prisons the opportunities for a person to learn a useful trade are negligible or nonexistent. Warehousing a person not only increases his bitterness, but makes it almost impossible for him to function usefully after he returns to society.

We can't ignore the fact that a percentage of our

population is made up of habitual and violent criminals, and for them I think a different approach is absolutely necessary. Frankly, we haven't yet found the solution to criminal incorrigibility, and for that reason I think such persons must be separated from the rest of society and not allowed to return.

It is also clear that indeterminate sentences and "resentencing" by the parole boards do much to increase the bitterness and sense of futility of prisoners. This would also eliminate the public's concern that some criminals spend too little time and some too much time in prison.

Most of these thoughts are not new. Many other men and women are deeply concerned with the need for reform in our prison system. Unfortunately, the prison society has no constituency. It is a cry for help that cannot be heard. But if we Christians are at all aware of our heritage, we will realize that we have no choice but to demand that county, state and federal governments put an end to such an outrageous degradation of human life.

One of the things I am beginning to realize is that Christians ought to have more of an impact on society. By that I don't mean that every Christian should run for public office—because not every Christian is cut out to serve the public. Nor do I believe that Christians should necessarily go out and vote for other Christians. I think we should vote for the person best qualified for the office, no matter what his or her religious beliefs. What I'm talking about is something much more basic than public office, and that is Christians ministering as Christians wherever there is human need. I'm talking about Christian individuals, groups, and churches reaching out into their communities with a Christlike love —bringing meals to the elderly and the shut-ins, operating coffee houses for youngsters, establishing

Gail is the author of *A Gift of Love,* her personal story of the Watergate events, and their effect on her life and that of the family.

Jeb and the children in St. Louis

Justin and Whitney

Stuart with Cinder, a year-old Bernese Mountain dog, the seventh member of the family. *Paul Rey photos*

homes for runaways, hospitals for those who are ill and can't afford medical care, housing for the dispossessed.

A church that seems to model this type of Christian concern is The Church of the Saviour in Washington, D.C. founded by Gordon Cosby. Membership there is not just open for the asking. Instead, each potential new member spends two years in serious study and in service programs designed to help participants discover their gifts and what is God's call upon their lives. Preparation for membership also includes participation in other significant areas of community life, such as corporate worship and retreat. Those who have completed the five approved classes and have been participating in a mission group of the church may make application for membership.

There is so much need in the world! It's not enough for us to introduce Christ to those who haven't met him and then go on our way. That isn't what Christ himself would do, and we know that from reading the Gospels. When Christ takes someone's hand, he holds onto it for all time. He really gets to know the person. He shares every pain, every spasm of fear, every crushed hope, self-accusation, and regret. So when Christ loves a person, it isn't a generalized, one-size-fits-all kind of love. It's a personal, direct, specific love that embraces all of a person's virtues and faults—and the person realizes that. He knows he is known, and he knows he is loved—and that makes a difference.

It's a difference that can change our world.

I want to put my time into the things I learned are most important in life—my God; my family (not only my direct family, but the extended family); and the work God has for me to do. I guess you could say that I want to find out what it means to *be* a Christian.